Excel
Get the Results You [Want]

Years 3–4
Opportunity Class
Mathematical
Reasoning Tests

**Allyn Jones
& Alan Horsfield**

PASCAL
PRESS

© 2022 Allyn Jones, Alan Horsfield and Pascal Press

Completely new edition incorporating 2021 Opportunity Class test changes

Reprinted 2024 (twice)

ISBN 978 1 74125 709 0

Pascal Press Pty Ltd
PO Box 250
Glebe NSW 2037
(02) 9198 1748
www.pascalpress.com.au

Publisher: Vivienne Joannou
Project editor: Rosemary Peers
Edited by Rosemary Peers
Proofread by Barbara Bessant and Mark Dixon
Answers checked by Peter Little
Cover by DiZign Pty Ltd
Typeset by Grizzly Graphics (Leanne Richters) and lj Design (Julianne Billington)
Printed by Vivar Printing/Green Giant Press

Contents

Sample tests

Answers

ABOUT THE OPPORTUNITY CLASS TEST

The NSW Opportunity Class Placement Test is required for placement in an Opportunity Class in a NSW public school.

This type of class offers an extra challenge for academically gifted students with high potential in Years 5 and 6. Selection is based on academic merit.

Students are usually in Year 4 when they apply for opportunity class placement and take the test.

Details are available at: https://education.nsw.gov.au.

The tests were updated in 2021 with a greater emphasis on literacy, thinking skills, mathematical reasoning and problem solving. The General Ability Test has been replaced by a Thinking Skills Test. The new NSW Opportunity Class Placement Test adjusts and balances the weighting given to the Reading, Thinking Skills and Mathematical Reasoning components; these are now equal. These changes were in response to the findings of the 2018 Review of Selective Education Access report, commissioned by the NSW Department of Education.

The NSW Opportunity Class Placement Test consists of three multiple-choice sections:

- **Reading** (25 questions in 30 minutes)
- **Mathematical Reasoning** (35 questions in 40 minutes)
- **Thinking Skills** (30 questions in 30 minutes).

Mathematical Reasoning test

The NSW Opportunity Class Placement Test includes a Mathematical Reasoning component.

What kinds of questions will be in the test?

All tests use multiple-choice questions where you have to choose the best answer from the five options.

What mathematics topics will be covered in the test?

The tests include questions involving Number, Patterns, Measurement, Geometry, Statistics, Probability and Working Mathematically. This means you will be familiar with the topics covered in the test but the questions may be more difficult or of a type you may not have seen before.

Do I have to study these areas before the test?

No. The best preparation is to know what to expect on the day of the test and to practise the types of questions in the test.

What kinds of questions will I be asked?

You will be given some information and asked one question about it. The information might be given in words or might involve a diagram, graph or table. You will be familiar with most question types from classroom work and from other tests you have done, such as the NAPLAN tests.

Do I have to answer all the questions?

Yes, you should try to answer every question. However, it is possible you will not have time to do them all. Some questions will take less than one minute to answer, while others will take longer. You will have to work quite quickly to answer all the questions. Many students don't manage to do this.

How can I make the best use of my time?

Here are a few tips to help you get through the test and to make the best use of your time.

- Don't waste too much time on any one question. If you aren't sure, guess the answer but mark it so you can come back to it later (if you have time). If it seems impossible to choose, select the answer you first thought was right.

- Answer every question. Don't leave any out. You have a chance of getting the right answer even if you guess.

- If you have time to spare, go over your answers. Sometimes you will realise the correct answer to a question after answering other questions.

Advice to students

Each question in the NSW Opportunity Class Placement Test is multiple choice. This means you have to choose the correct answer from the given options.

We have included sample answer sheets in this book for you to practise on. Note that from 2025, however, the NSW Opportunity Class Placement Test will change to a computer-based test.

Some of the more challenging Thinking Skills problem-solving questions could take you up to 10 minutes to complete to begin with, as you may use diagrams or tables to help you solve them. Remember that the more questions you do of this same type, the faster you will become — until you know exactly how to solve them.

Mathematical Reasoning answer sheet

Mark your answers here.

To answer each question, fill in the appropriate circle for your chosen answer.

Use a pencil. If you make a mistake or change your mind, erase and try again.

You can make extra copies of this answer sheet to mark your answers to all the Sample Mathematical Reasoning tests in this book.

	A B C D E		A B C D E		A B C D E		A B C D E		A B C D E
1	○○○○○	8	○○○○○	15	○○○○○	22	○○○○○	29	○○○○○
2	○○○○○	9	○○○○○	16	○○○○○	23	○○○○○	30	○○○○○
3	○○○○○	10	○○○○○	17	○○○○○	24	○○○○○	31	○○○○○
4	○○○○○	11	○○○○○	18	○○○○○	25	○○○○○	32	○○○○○
5	○○○○○	12	○○○○○	19	○○○○○	26	○○○○○	33	○○○○○
6	○○○○○	13	○○○○○	20	○○○○○	27	○○○○○	34	○○○○○
7	○○○○○	14	○○○○○	21	○○○○○	28	○○○○○	35	○○○○○

SAMPLE TEST 1

1 The number in each of the squares is the result of multiplying the numbers in the nearest circles.

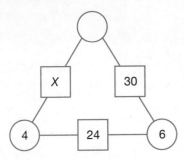

For example, in the bottom row, 4 × 6 = 24. What is the number represented by the letter *X*?

9	20	16	24	32
A	B	C	D	E

2 Ethan buys two pens that cost $3.70 each. How much change will he receive from a $10 note?

A $2.40

B $2.60

C $3.40

D $3.60

E $6.30

3 Which number goes in the empty box to complete this number pattern?

4	0	8	12	?
14	2	26	38	23

3	5	7	13	16
A	B	C	D	E

4 Four friends meet after a holiday. They all shake hands once with each other.
How many handshakes do they have altogether?

6	8	10	16	15
A	B	C	D	E

5
```
  4 5 8
− 1 □ 3
───────
  2 9 5
```
To make the subtraction correct, the □ should be replaced with

0	4	5	6	7
A	B	C	D	E

6 Luke was given this number puzzle. He has to find the number that started the puzzle.

START → +7 → ×3 → ANSWER 36

What number should Luke start with to get the answer given?

5	9	10	26	19
A	B	C	D	E

7 Tom raised $33 in a school read-a-thon. He has to collect the money.
This is his list of the money he has collected.

Mr James	$5
Uncle Bob	$2
Mrs Michaels.	$8
Ms Hawke	$1
Peter Bray	$6
Grandpa.	? ? ?

How much should Grandpa pay Tom?

$1	$10	$11	$12	$5
A	B	C	D	E

8 When I triple 11, then take one dozen away, what number do I have?

21	22	23	24	25
A	B	C	D	E

9 Which of these numbers is closest to 700?

690	709	800	721	770
A	B	C	D	E

10 The grocer is selling oranges for 90c each. What is the greatest number of oranges that can be purchased with a $10 note?

9	10	11	12	14
A	B	C	D	E

11 Which of these numbers has the smallest number of factors?

A 4

B 8

C 12

D 14

E 17

12 Ella baked a cake. She cut it into two equal pieces and gave one of the pieces to her friend. She then cut her piece into four equal pieces. If Ella gave one of these pieces to her mother, what fraction of the original cake did her mother receive?

A one-fifth

B one-sixth

C one-eighth

D three-eighths

E one-quarter

13 Aiden has half as many balls as Lily. Lily has eight more balls than Jacob who has two fewer balls than Elijah. If Elijah has 16 balls, how many balls has Aiden?

A 6

B 8

C 10

D 11

E 12

14 How many eggs are in seven and a half dozen?

A 10

B 75

C 76

D 89

E 90

15 In this diagram, $4 \times 2 = 8$.

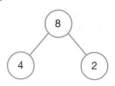

Here is a new diagram that works in the same way.

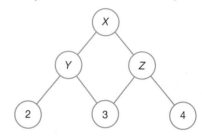

What is the value of X?

6	12	36	60	72
A	B	C	D	E

16 Russell is on a driving holiday. At an intersection he comes to this sign.

How much closer is Bald Hill than Dry Creek?

A 17 km

B 19 km

C 29 km

D 53 km

E 21 km

17 Logan paints three walls each with dimensions 4 m by 3 m. Each litre of his paint covers 2 m². How much paint will Logan use?

6 L	18 L	20 L	24 L	36 L
A	B	C	D	E

SAMPLE TEST 1

18 Which of these groups of 2D shapes could be used to form a square pyramid?

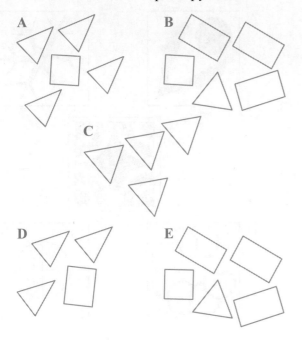

19 A tap is dripping water into a bucket. The tap drips a drop every 3 seconds. If each drop is 1 mL, how much water is in the bucket after one hour?

A 60 mL

B 120 mL

C 600 mL

D 900 mL

E 1200 mL

20 Gladys arranged these masses from lightest to heaviest.

120 g   1.3 kg   87 g   1.004 kg   769 g

Which mass is in the middle of her list?

A 120 g

B 1.3 kg

C 87 g

D 1.004 kg

E 769 g

21 There are 25 students enrolled in Mr Robinson's Year 4 class. He asked his students how many siblings they had in their families. Some students were absent from the class at the time. The results are shown in the graph.

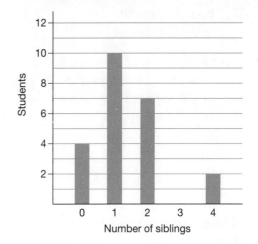

George reads the graph and makes three claims:

1 Four students have two siblings.

2 Nine students have more than one sibling.

3 There were two students absent.

Using the information on the graph, which of George's claims is/are correct?

A claim 1 only   B claim 2 only

C claim 3 only   D claims 1 and 3 only

E claims 2 and 3 only

22 Ava is doing this puzzle.

Write the same whole number in each triangle to make the number sentences true.

▲ + ▲ is less than 16.

12 + ▲ is bigger than 15.

Ava noticed that there is more than one correct answer to the puzzle.

How many different correct answers are there?

2	3	4	5	6
A	B	C	D	E

23 Ms Ho leaves home for school at 6:55 am and enters her classroom at 8:22 am. How long is her trip to school?

A 27 minutes

B 33 minutes

C 1 hour 17 minutes

D 1 hour 27 minutes

E 1 hour 33 minutes

24 Scott buys 250 g of cherries, half a kilogram of strawberries and 700 g of peaches. What is the total mass?

A 955 g

B 1000 g

C 1350 g

D 1450 g

E 1550 g

25 A large square with an area of 50 cm^2 is drawn on a grid. A shaded square is drawn inside the large square.

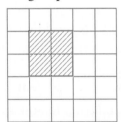

What is the area of the shaded square?

4 cm^2	8 cm^2	12 cm^2	16 cm^2	24 cm^2
A	B	C	D	E

26 How many triangles are there in this star shape?

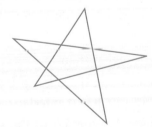

5	8	10	11	7
A	B	C	D	E

27 Which one of these designs **not** have a line of symmetry?

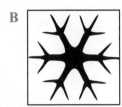

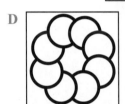 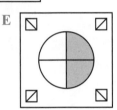

28 Jordan started to watch a movie at 7:55 pm. The movie ran for 132 minutes. When did the movie finish?

A 9:27 pm

B 10:07 pm

C 9:37 pm

D 9:17 pm

E 10:17 pm

29 Josh has these coloured pencils in his pencil case.

1 red	2 green
2 blue	1 black
3 yellow	1 pink

He takes one pencil out without looking. What is the chance that it is a yellow pencil?

A 1 chance in 3

B 1 chance in 10

C 3 chances in 7

D 3 chances in 10

E 1 chance in 6

30 An orange was cut as shown.

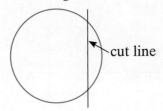

The shape of the face where the orange has been cut will be most like:

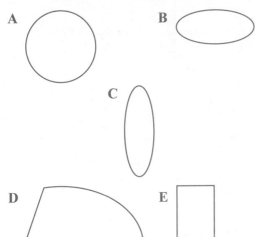

A
B
C
D
E

31 This is a triangular prism.

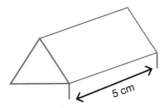

The ends are 3-cm equilateral triangles.
Its length is 5 cm.
What is the total length of all the edges?
A 19 cm
B 24 cm
C 28 cm
D 33 cm
E 14 cm

32 Sarah is shading squares on the grid so that the vertical and horizontal lines are lines of symmetry. She needs to shade three more squares. What are the grid references of the three squares?

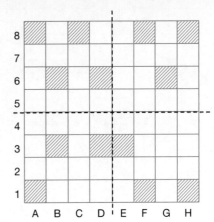

A C2, G3, E6
B C1, G4, E6
C B1, G3, D6
D B1, G4, D6
E C1, G3, E6

33 Cindy needs to finish making this stack of 9 blocks into a cube.

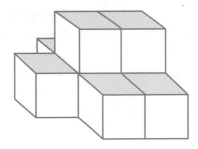

What is the **least** number of blocks she needs to make the stack into a cube?

9	18	21	22	7
A	B	C	D	E

34 The graph shows the temperatures recorded during a day in Penrith.

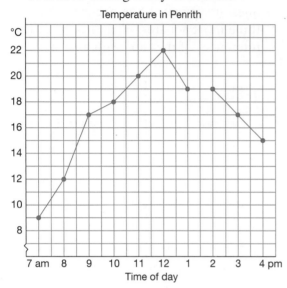

Lara reads the graph and makes three claims:

1 The temperature at 4 pm was higher than the temperature at 9 am.

2 The temperature at 7 am was half the temperature at 10 am.

3 From 8 am the temperature increased by 10 degrees over a 4-hour period.

Using the information on the graph, which of Lara's claims is/are correct?

A claim 1 only
B claim 2 only
C claims 1 and 3 only
D claims 2 and 3 only
E claims 1, 2 and 3

35 The grid shows the homes of six friends: Abby, Bart, Chloe, Drew, Ella and Fred.

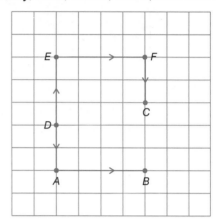

On Saturday morning, Drew left his home and walked to Abby's home then to Bart's home. This was a distance of 300 m. On Sunday morning, he left his home again and visited Ella, then Fred and then Chloe. How far did he walk on Sunday morning?

A 900 m
B 600 m
C 540 m
D 500 m
E 450 m

SAMPLE TEST 2

1 Which number is 4 hundreds less than 16 257?

A 16 227

B 16 057

C 15 957

D 13 257

E 15 857

2 Brittany has a jar containing 50-cent coins and 20-cent coins. The total amount of money is $4.20. If there are four 50-cent coins, how many 20-cent coins are in the jar?

5	6	9	11	16
A	B	C	D	E

3 I purchased six dozen eggs. Seven were broken.

How many eggs remained unbroken?

53	65	67	79	57
A	B	C	D	E

4 Barry has started putting beads onto this abacus. He has to show the number 17 158.

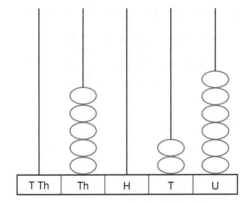

He will have to put the **most** extra beads onto the

A units (ones) spike.

B tens spike.

C hundreds spike.

D thousands spike.

E ten-thousands spike.

5 Ginger has these coins.

She has

A $1.60   B $1.75   C $1.80

D $1.55   E $1.70

6 What is the total of the multiples of three between ten and twenty?

25	27	35	37	45
A	B	C	D	E

7 What fraction of this shape is shaded?

$\frac{7}{9}$	$\frac{1}{2}$	$\frac{2}{3}$	$\frac{7}{16}$	$\frac{3}{4}$
A	B	C	D	E

8 Rita has to finish this magic addition square.

2	9	X
7	5	
6	1	8

Which number should replace the *X*?

2	4	6	8	3
A	B	C	D	E

SAMPLE TEST 2

9 Which is the next number in this series?

60, 59, 57, 54, 50 …

49	46	45	40	44
A	B	C	D	E

10 Kylie is reading a book with 32 pages. It has a picture on the second page. There is a picture every third page after that. How many pages have pictures on them?

9	10	11	12	13
A	B	C	D	E

11 The Brooks family have two tricycles and three skateboards. Which of these will give the total number of wheels?

A $3 + 2 \times 5$

B $5 \times 4 + 3$

C $4 \times 3 + 3 \times 3$

D $2 \times 3 + 3 \times 4$

E $2 + 2 + 2 + 3 + 3 + 3$

12 Which of these road signs has **no** line of symmetry?

13 How many rectangles, of any size, are there in this shape?

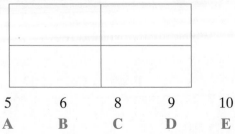

5	6	8	9	10
A	B	C	D	E

14 This star always represents the same number.
What number does it stand for in this number sentence?

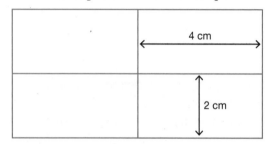

5	6	19	20	4
A	B	C	D	E

15 This shape is made up of 4 rectangles. They are all 4 cm long and 2 cm wide. What is the perimeter of the shape?

	← 4 cm →
	↕ 2 cm

A 24 cm   B 28 cm   C 32 cm

D 48 cm   E 56 cm

16 At Pizza Palace, the Tan family bought three pizzas. Mr Tan ate $\frac{3}{4}$ of a pizza. Mrs Tan had $\frac{1}{4}$ of a pizza, Tammy had $\frac{1}{2}$ of a pizza and Fiona had $\frac{3}{4}$ of a pizza. How much pizza was left over?

A none

B $\frac{1}{4}$ of a pizza   C $\frac{1}{2}$ of a pizza

D $\frac{3}{4}$ of a pizza   E $1\frac{1}{4}$ pizzas

17 Three 4-cm squares are arranged as shown to make this shape.

They each overlap halfway along the side of the adjacent square.
What is the perimeter of the shape?

A 36 cm   B 38 cm   C 40 cm

D 42 cm   E 44 cm

18 Here is a number pattern.

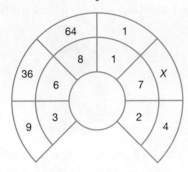

What number should go in the space marked with *X*?

14	21	28	42	49
A	B	C	D	E

19 Yuri cut this cylinder in half, as shown by the dotted line.

Which shape looks most like the face made by the cut?

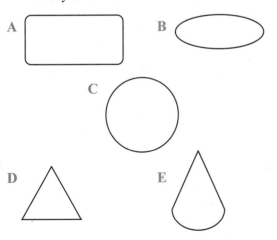

20 Jessica had a piece of cardboard 6 cm × 5 cm. She pasted a picture on it, which left a 1-cm border around the picture.

What is the size of Jessica's picture?
A 7 cm × 8 cm   **B** 5 cm × 4 cm
C 6 cm × 4 cm   **D** 4 cm × 3 cm
E 6 cm × 3 cm

21 Tina counts the number of halves in 8. Sean counts the number of thirds in 6. What is the difference between the two counts?

1	2	3	4	5
A	B	C	D	E

22 This diagram shows the fuel gauge of a car. When the tank is full it holds 60 L. About how many litres of fuel are in the tank?

A 5 L   **B** 15 L   **C** 25 L
D 30 L   **E** 45 L

23 Louise bought six cakes, each at the same price. She paid using a $20 note. She received $5 in change. What was the cost of each cake?

A $1.50

B $1.75

C $2.25

D $2.45

E $2.50

24 Carol Street School raised money in a read-a-thon. A graph was drawn to show how much each year group raised.

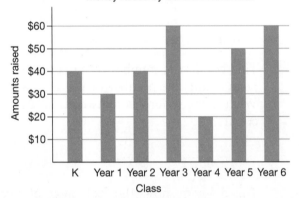

How much money was raised by K, Year 1 and Year 2 altogether?

A $11

B $40

C $100

D $110

E $170

25 Sam has a bag of 20 marbles. There are 10 red marbles and 10 green marbles.

Without looking, he takes a marble from his bag. What is the chance it will be a red marble?

A 1 in 2

B 1 in 5

C 1 in 10

D 1 in 20

E 1 in 4

26 What fraction of this shape is shaded?

A five-sevenths

B seven-tenths

C five-sixths

D one-half

E five-twelfths

27 1 January is a Saturday.
What day will 1 February be?

A Saturday

B Sunday

C Monday

D Tuesday

E Wednesday

28 Elsie had 28 coins. A quarter of the coins were $2 coins and the remainder $1. What was the total amount of money?

A $28

B $30

C $32

D $35

E $36

29 John has been putting blocks on a balance beam.

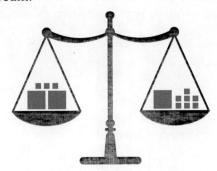

The large blocks all have the same mass.
Each small block has a mass of 250 g.
What is the mass of each large block?

A 500 g
B 1.25 kg
C 2.5 kg
D 4000 g
E 1 kg

30 This is a floor plan of Tanya's bedroom.

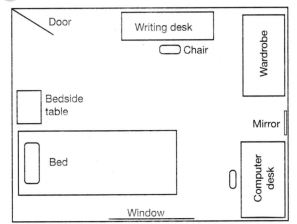

Tanya's bed is about 1 m wide.
From the doorway to the window is about

A 2 m
B 3 m
C 5 m
D 6 m
E 7 m

31 Ken was born on 5 June 1988. How old was he in January 2017?

28	29	31	37	38
A	**B**	**C**	**D**	**E**

32 This is a treasure map of Turtle Island.

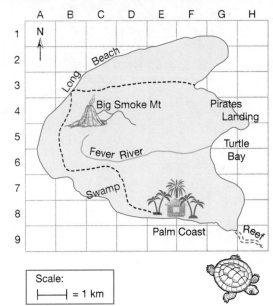

To get from the hut at Palm Coast to Big Smoke Mt, I would have to travel in a

A north-easterly direction.
B north-westerly direction.
C south-westerly direction.
D south-easterly direction.
E southerly direction.

33 Marty drew this design using rectangles.

How many right angles are in this shape?

8	12	16	18	20
A	**B**	**C**	**D**	**E**

34 How many small cubes are in this shape?

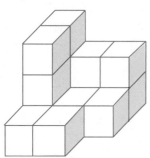

A 10
B 13
C 14
D 16
E 17

35 All the junior members at a sports club made a graph of their favourite sport. Each square represents two members.

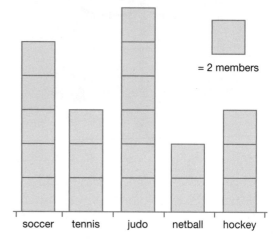

= 2 members

soccer   tennis   judo   netball   hockey

How many members were in the survey?

6	19	20	38	40
A	B	C	D	E

SAMPLE TEST 3

1
   157
    98
+ □6
  281

What number should the □ be replaced with to make the addition correct?

1	2	3	4	5
A	B	C	D	E

2 What is the product of the even numbers **between** 5 and 10?

2	14	40	48	54
A	B	C	D	E

3 Robert had $10. He spent $2.35 on an ice cream and $1.75 on an energy drink. How much change should he have?

A $4.10   **B** $5.85   **C** $5.80
D $6.00   **E** $5.90

4 What is the next number after 40 that is a multiple of three and four?

42	44	46	48	52
A	B	C	D	E

5 Here is a crossword puzzle.

P	L	U	R	A	L	
E						P
R	E	L	A	P	S	E
U		O				T
S	Q	U	A	L	O	R
E		S				O
	R	E	P	E	A	L

What fraction of the puzzle is made up of black squares?

A about one-half
B about one-third
C about one-quarter
D about one-tenth
E about one-seventh

6 A shape is made from squares.

Three-fifths of the shape is shaded. How many squares will be shaded?

3	6	8	9	12
A	B	C	D	E

7

What is the time 435 minutes later?

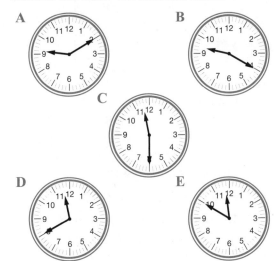

8 Which group of coins totals $2.85?

A

B

C

D

E

9 The two puzzles use the same rule.

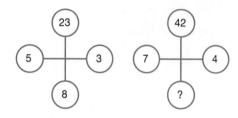

What is the missing number?

6	35	17	26	14
A	B	C	D	E

10 In this magic square, numbers in each row, column and diagonal add to the same number.

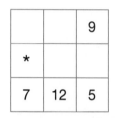

What is the value of the *?

11	4	8	10	6
A	B	C	D	E

11 This is a number series.

1, 2, 6, 24, ♠, 720

To complete the series, which number should replace the ♠ ?

48	96	120	192	240
A	B	C	D	E

12 Sophia buys a punnet of strawberries costing $2.40. She uses a $5 note to pay for the strawberries. What is the smallest number of coins she can be given as change?

2	3	4	5	6
A	B	C	D	E

13 ☐ − 12 + 9 = 19
☐ =

0	21	22	40	16
A	B	C	D	E

14 In February the top temperature was: In August the top temperature was:

What was the difference in temperature?

20 °C	22 °C	26 °C	32 °C	39 °C
A	B	C	D	E

15 Which number comes next in this series?

1, 1, 2, 6, 24 …

24	31	48	120	96
A	B	C	D	E

16 Which shape covers the most area?

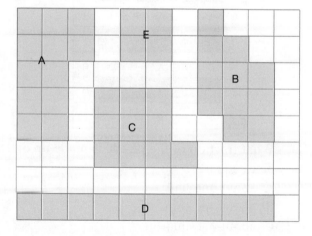

SAMPLE TEST 3

17 4M conducted a survey to find out which months had the most birthdays. They used their survey information to make this graph.

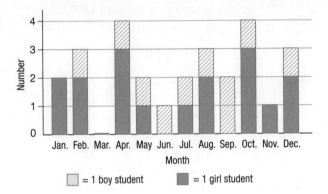

Which statement is correct?

A Four girls have birthdays in April.

B There are girls' birthdays in every month.

C April is the only month when three girls have a birthday.

D Most birthdays are in the second half of the year.

E The season with the most birthdays is spring.

18 Ian wrote numbers on these cards. He then shuffled them and turned them face down.

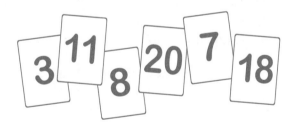

He selects one card. What are the chances it is a card with an even number on it?

A 1 chance in 6

B 1 chance in 5

C 3 chances in 5

D 5 chances in 6

E 1 chance in 2

19 The length of this rectangle is twice as long as its width.

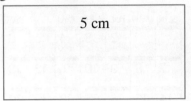

What is the perimeter of this rectangle?

A 7.5 cm   B 10 cm

C 12.5 cm   D 15 cm

E 20 cm

Questions 20, 21 and 22 refer to the following Thai Fish Salad recipe.

Jill has this recipe card for Thai Fish Salad.

INGREDIENTS   (Serves 4)

2 tablespoons salad oil

500 g fresh tuna, cut into cubes

8 fresh asparagus spears

200 g lettuce leaves

12 cherry tomatoes, cut into quarters

1 cucumber, sliced

450 g tin of baby corn

20 The cherry tomatoes have to be cut into quarters to make Thai Fish Salad. How many quarters will be used in the Thai Fish Salad altogether?

3	15	24	48	36
A	B	C	D	E

21 Jill wants to make enough Thai Fish Salad for six people.
How many asparagus spears will she need?

12	14	16	18	10
A	B	C	D	E

22 Last week, Jill made the Thai Fish Salad for four people. She opened a 1 kg tin of baby corn. What mass of baby corn was not used in the Thai Fish Salad?

50 g	450 g	550 g	650 g	955 g
A	B	C	D	E

23 Mrs Grace goes to work every weekday in June. Monday 8 June was a holiday.

SUN	MON	TUE	WED	THU	FRI	SAT
		1	2	3	4	5	6
7	8	9	10	11	12	13
14	15	16	17	18	19	20
21	22	23	24	25	26	27
28	29	30				

How many days did she work in June?

19	21	22	30	27
A	B	C	D	E

24 In this calculation each letter always stands for the same digit.

$$W + W + W = XW$$

To make the calculation correct, W stands for

1	4	5	7	2
A	B	C	D	E

25 Rowan has drawn a 2D shape. It has:
- four sides
- opposite sides which are the same length
- no right angles.

It is a

A kite.

B triangle.

C rectangle.

D parallelogram.

E hexagon.

26 A hiker starts a walk by heading south. He does a left turn before coming to a river. He turns left again to follow the river bank. In what direction is he now walking?

A a northerly direction

B a southerly direction

C an easterly direction

D a westerly direction

E a north-westerly direction

27 The smaller angle between the hands of a clock at 5 o'clock is

A an angle less than 90°.

B a right angle.

C an angle between 90° and 180°.

D an angle greater than 180°.

E an angle measuring 180°.

28 The difference between the number of faces and the number of edges of a hexagonal prism is

0	8	10	12	12
A	B	C	D	E

29 This year Andy's birthday is on a Saturday. He is 13 days older than Beth. Esther is 19 days older than Beth. What day of the week is Esther's birthday this year?

A Friday

B Thursday

C Saturday

D Monday

E Sunday

30 How many litres are in 2500 mL?

A 2.5

B 25

C 250

D 25 000

E 2 500 000

31 This is the top view of one 3D shape sitting on top of another 3D shape.

Which pair of 3D shapes could it be?

A a triangular prism on a cone

B a square pyramid on a cube

C a rectangular prism on a cylinder

D a triangular pyramid on a triangular prism

E a triangular prism on a cube

SAMPLE TEST 3

32 I rotate this shape a quarter of a turn clockwise three times.

How will it now appear?

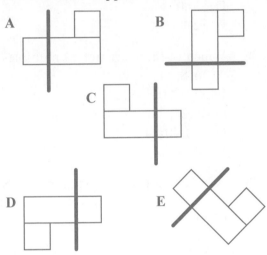

33 On a treasure map, a distance of 8 km is represented as a length of 4 cm. If the distance from a goldmine to a dead tree is 6 km, how far apart are they on the map?

A 5 cm

B 4 cm

C 3 cm

D 2 cm

E 12 cm

34 Liam, Ethan and Olivia are comparing their ages. Liam is two-thirds the age of Ethan and four-fifths the age of Olivia. If Ethan is 24 years old, how old is Olivia?

A 16

B 18

C 20

D 21

E 30

35 The numbers of books read by five students are recorded in the graph below.

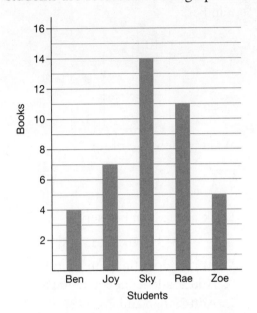

Carol reads the graph and makes three claims:

1 Joy read three more books than Ben.

2 Sky read more books than Rae and Zoe together.

3 Joy read half as many books as Sky.

Using the information on the graph, which of Carol's claims is/are correct?

A claim 1 only

B claim 2 only

C claim 3 only

D claims 1 and 3 only

E claims 1, 2 and 3 only

1 In this magic square, numbers in each row, column and diagonal add to the same number.

10		
	7	9
	*	4

What is the value of the *?

11	5	8	12	6
A	B	C	D	E

2 Look at this number series.

3, 5, 8, 10, 13, 15, 18

What rule does the pattern follow?
A Add 2, add 3, then add 3 again.
B Add 2, then add 3.
C Double, then subtract 1.
D Add 2, then 3, then 4, and so on.
E Add 3, then add 2.

3 Brett has 17 sports cards and Andre has 10 times as many. How many sports cards do they have altogether?

7	27	170	187	197
A	B	C	D	E

4 Lucy was given this number puzzle. She has to find the number that started the puzzle.

| START | → | × 5 | → | − 3 | → | Answer 22 |

What number should Lucy start with to get the answer given?

2	5	8	26	125
A	B	C	D	E

5 The length of a rectangle is twice its width. If the perimeter is 24 cm, what is the area of the rectangle?
A 20 cm²
B 24 cm²
C 32 cm²
D 64 cm²
E 128 cm²

6 A supermarket sells small bags of lemons for $2.10. There are six lemons in each bag. Halle buys two dozen lemons. How much change will she receive from a $10 note?
A $0.80
B $1.40
C $1.60
D $1.80
E $2.40

7 Which of these are **not** all multiples of 4?
A 16, 8, 44
B 32, 4, 20
C 48, 36, 28
D 100, 40, 24
E 24, 20, 14

8 A cake is cut into 12 equal pieces. Spiro eats two pieces. What fraction of the cake remains?

$\frac{1}{10}$	$\frac{1}{6}$	$\frac{2}{3}$	$\frac{5}{6}$	$\frac{2}{11}$
A	B	C	D	E

9 Here is a diagram with seven circles arranged in columns and rows. The numbers 1 to 7 are written in the circles so that the sums of the three numbers in each line are the same.

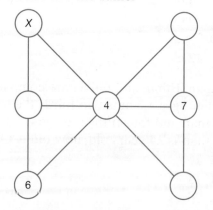

What number replaces the letter *X*?

1	2	3	4	5
A	B	C	D	E

10 Tony made this number using an abacus. He then took one bead off each spike.

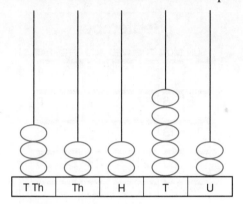

| T Th | Th | H | T | U |

What is his new number?

A twenty-two thousand, one hundred and forty-one

B twenty-two thousand, one hundred and fifty-one

C twenty-one thousand, one hundred and fifty-two

D twenty-one thousand, one hundred and forty-one

E twenty-one thousand, two hundred and forty-one

11 Mrs Scott buys bowls for the school canteen. She can buy two bowls for $5. How many bowls could she buy for $75?

15	30	45	50	7
A	B	C	D	E

12 Justin had $60. He bought six tickets for the cinema at $8.50 each.
How much change did he receive?

A $9

B $10

C $10.50

D $11.50

E $12

13 Which is the missing number in this series?

268, 259, ☐, 241, 232, 223, 214

250	251	252	253	249
A	B	C	D	E

14 One-third of the passengers on a bus are children. There are 24 passengers on the bus. How many adults are on the bus?

6	18	12	8	16
A	B	C	D	E

15 Gianna is making a necklace. For every three blue beads, she uses two red beads and a white bead. If there are 54 beads in the necklace, how many are red?

6	8	12	18	20
A	B	C	D	E

16 Tessa wants to complete this number sentence correctly.

$$\square - 9 = 15 + 4$$

She should replace the ☐ with

9	10	19	20	28
A	B	C	D	E

17 What is the perimeter of this shape?

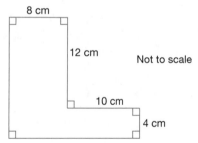

8 cm

12 cm

Not to scale

10 cm

4 cm

A 50 cm

B 34 cm

C 52 cm

D 72 cm

E 68 cm

18 Edward steps on a set of bathroom scales. His mass is 38 kg. His father's mass is two-and-a-half times Edward's mass. What is the mass of Edward's father?

A 57 kg

B 76 kg

C 85 kg

D 89 kg

E 95 kg

19 Tony's watch doesn't have numbers on the dial. What is the time shown on his watch?

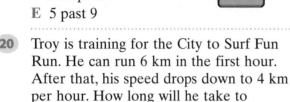

A 20 to 7
B half past 9
C a quarter to 6
D half past 8
E 5 past 9

20 Troy is training for the City to Surf Fun Run. He can run 6 km in the first hour. After that, his speed drops down to 4 km per hour. How long will he take to complete the 14 km run?

A 2 hours
B 2 hours thirty minutes
C 3 hours
D 3 hours thirty minutes
E 4 hours

21 Karen opens a 1.25 L bottle of soft drink. She has a set of six glasses, each of which holds 250 mL. How many glasses can she completely fill?

2	3	4	5	6
A	B	C	D	E

22 The diagram below shows a pan balance.

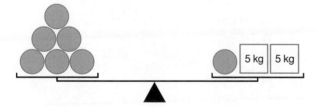

What is the total mass of 2 balls?
A 4 kg
B 2 kg
C 3 kg
D 5 kg
E 10 kg

23 Today is 14 September. Joel's wedding anniversary was three weeks ago.

September						
SUN	MON	TUE	WED	THU	FRI	SAT
			1	2	3	4
5	6	7	8	9	10	11
12	13	14	15	16	17	18
19	20	21	22	23	24	25
26	27	28	29	30		

What was the date of his anniversary?
A 21 August
B 22 August
C 23 August
D 24 August
E 25 August

24 Steven dropped his plate and a piece broke off.

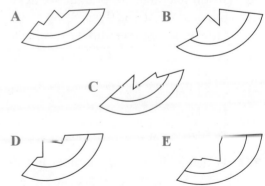

Which piece was part of Steven's plate?

A   B

C

D   E

SAMPLE TEST 4

Questions 25 to 28 refer to the map of Lakemba Island (Fiji).

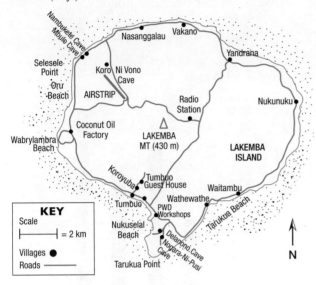

Mr and Mrs Ryan and their two children, Amy and George, go to Lakemba Island for a holiday. They stay at the Guest House in Tumbuo.

25 The AIRSTRIP is
A north of Oru Beach.
B south of Oru Beach.
C east of Oru Beach.
D west of Oru Beach.
E south-east of Oru Beach.

26 The distance from the Coconut Oil Factory to Tarukua Beach is about
A 2 km.
B 4 km.
C 6 km.
D 8 km.
E 12 km.

27 Lakemba Mt is about
A half a kilometre high.
B a kilometre high.
C four kilometres high.
D four and a half kilometres high.
E nine kilometres high.

28 It takes George and Amy fifteen minutes to walk from the Guest House to Tarukua Beach.
If they arrived at the beach at 1:05 pm, what time did they leave the Guest House?
A 1:20 pm
B 12:20 am
C 12:50 pm
D 1:50 pm
E 10:05 am

29 Duane is doing this puzzle.
Write the same whole number in each circle to make the number sentences true.

14 – ● is more than 5.

● + ● is bigger than 6.

Duane noticed that there is more than one correct answer to the puzzle.
How many different correct answers are there?

2	3	4	5	6
A	B	C	D	E

30 A group of people who were born in Australia were surveyed to find the state of their birth. Half the people were born in NSW. Twice as many people were born in Queensland than in Victoria. Those people born elsewhere are shown in the sector marked as 'Other'.

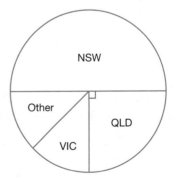

If eight people were born in Queensland, how many people were surveyed?

12	16	24	32	40
A	B	C	D	E

31 Melody has to complete the reflection of this shape on the right-hand side of the mirror line.

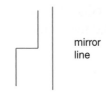

mirror line

The reflection should look like:

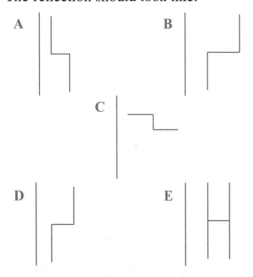

A B

C

D E

32 Here are four shapes.

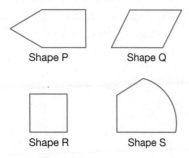

Shape P   Shape Q

Shape R   Shape S

Two shapes are chosen at random. What is the smallest possible number of right angles that can be counted on the **remaining** shapes?

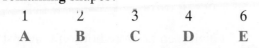

1	2	3	4	6
A	B	C	D	E

33 Sarah graphed the amount she spent each week on her overseas holiday.

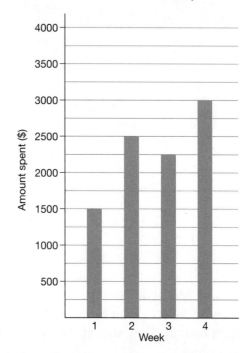

Ellie reads the graph and makes three claims:

1 Sarah spent $2250 in week 3.
2 Sarah spent $500 more in week 4 than in week 2.
3 Sarah spent a total of $6050 in weeks 1, 2 and 3.

Using the information on the graph, which of Ellie's claims is/are correct?

A claim 1 only
B claim 2 only
C claims 1 and 2 only
D claims 1 and 3 only
E claims 1, 2 and 3

34 Colin had these six numbered cards in a dark bag.

The chance of pulling out a card with an odd number on it is

A 1 chance in 2.

B 1 chance in 3.

C 1 chance in 6.

D 3 chances in 3.

E 3 chances in 5.

35 The diagram shows a shape consisting of three identical rectangles. Each rectangle measures 4 cm by 2 cm.

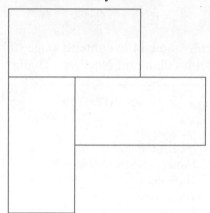

What is the perimeter of the shape?

A 16 cm

B 24 cm

C 28 cm

D 32 cm

E 36 cm

1 If I write the numbers from 1 to 20, how many times will I write numeral 1?

10	11	12	13	14
A	B	C	D	E

2 Joseph studied the contents page of a travel brochure on Northern Thailand.

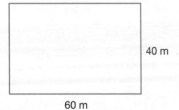

CONTENTS

Which section of the book uses the greatest number of pages?

A Temples of Chiang Mai
B Eating Out in Town
C Historic Monuments
D The People
E District Tours

3 The diagram shows a plan for a memorial park. The park is rectangular with side lengths 60 m by 40 m. Small trees are to be planted on the park's boundary. Trees are to be planted 20 m apart.

40 m

60 m

How many trees will be planted?

12	5	14	16	10
A	B	C	D	E

4 In this puzzle, numbers in opposite squares multiply together to give the number in the middle square.

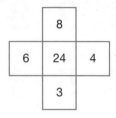

Here is another puzzle that follows the same rule.

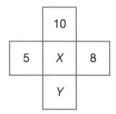

What is the difference between the numbers represented by X and Y?

28	32	36	40	44
A	B	C	D	E

5 I have these coins.

What is the least number of extra coins I need to have $10?

5	6	7	9	8
A	B	C	D	E

6 Kelsey has fewer than 50 beads in a jar. When she places them in groups of four or five she has none left over. But when she places them in groups of six she has four left over. What is the exact number of beads in the jar?

45	40	30	20	24
A	B	C	D	E

SAMPLE TEST 5

7 What is half of the sum of 12 and 18?

6	24	14	16	15
A	B	C	D	E

8 Elle has saved half as much again as her sister.
If Elle's sister has $12, what is the combined total of their savings?

$14	$18	$24	$30	$36
A	B	C	D	E

9 Symon has a bag of 80 golf balls and has decided to give them away. He gives half of the balls to Chloe. Hudson receives a quarter of the balls and Leo is given the rest. How many balls does Leo receive?

10	15	16	20	30
A	B	C	D	E

10 Helen held this shape in front of a mirror.

Which one of these is the reflection of Helen's shape?

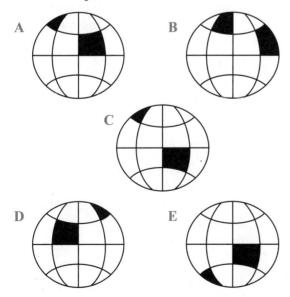

11 A rideshare company charges $4 for a call-out fee, plus $2 for every kilometre of a journey. What total amount will Andrea pay for a 10-km journey?

$16	$24	$26	$42	$60
A	B	C	D	E

12 How many quarters are in 6?

10	24	16	32	46
A	B	C	D	E

13 The number in each of the squares is the result of adding the numbers in the nearest circles.

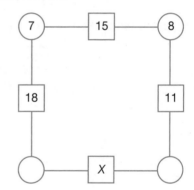

For example, in the top row $7 + 8 = 15$. What is the number represented by the letter X?

6	44	19	24	14
A	B	C	D	E

14 After winning a game of inter-school soccer Glen, Robert and Jim do a 'high five' once with each other.
How many times did they 'high five' with each other?

3	4	6	9	2
A	B	C	D	E

15 Which number would best replace the X in this number pattern?

105, 95, X, 78, 71, 65

84	85	86	87	88
A	B	C	D	E

16 When Harine drives her car 100 km, she uses 8 L. How far will she drive if she uses 20 L?

A 260 km

B 320 km

C 128 km

D 400 km

E 250 km

17 Which of these letters does **not** have a line of symmetry?

W	B	H	P	T
A	B	C	D	E

18 The diagram below shows a pan balance.

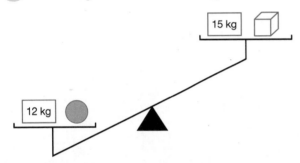

Which of these could be the mass of the ball and cube?

A mass of ball = 6 kg and mass of cube = 3 kg

B mass of ball = 6 kg and mass of cube = 6 kg

C mass of ball = 3 kg and mass of cube = 2 kg

D mass of ball = 3 kg and mass of cube = 6 kg

E mass of ball = 6 kg and mass of cube = 2 kg

19 To complete this number pattern, what number should go in the shaded box?

2	1	6	5	3
5	2	37		10

25	26	31	34	24
A	B	C	D	E

20 4 ☐ 4 ☐ 3 = 13

What are the two missing signs needed to make this number sentence correct?

A + and +

B + and ×

C × and +

D × and –

E × and ×

21 A rectangle and a square are both drawn on the grid below. The rectangle has a perimeter of 28 cm. What is the perimeter of the square?

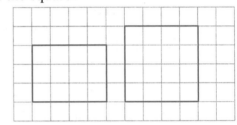

A 16 cm

B 24 cm

C 28 cm

D 32 cm

E 36 cm

22 The mass of an apple is 240 g. The mass of the apple and two oranges is 680 g. If the oranges have identical masses, what is the total mass of an apple and an orange?

A 440 g

B 460 g

C 470 g

D 480 g

E 490 g

23 On Friday 13 June, Karen was given a class project to do. She had to hand it in 20 days later.

On which day was her project due?

A Thursday

B Wednesday

C Tuesday

D Monday

E Sunday

SAMPLE TEST 5

24 A decagon is a 2D shape with 10 sides. How many edges has a decagonal prism?

36	20	28	24	30
A	B	C	D	E

25 A train left Albury station at 10:40 am and arrived at Central station at 7:15 pm. How long was the train trip?

A 7 hours 25 minutes
B 7 hours 35 minutes
C 8 hours 25 minutes
D 8 hours 35 minutes
E 9 hours 35 minutes

26 Tegan drew some shapes on a piece of cardboard.

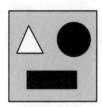

She then rotated her cardboard.
Which of these **cannot** be her sheet?

A 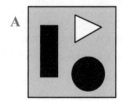   B

C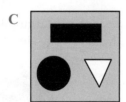

D 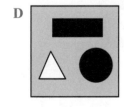   E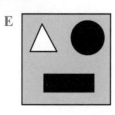

27 The graph shows the height of six students.

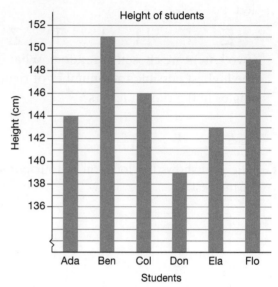

What is the difference in height between the tallest and shortest student?

A 13 cm   B 8 cm   C 9 cm
D 11 cm   E 12 cm

28 Mr Siros shares $3 equally between his four children. What is each child's share?

55c	65c	75c	85c	90c
A	B	C	D	E

29 Two identical rectangles with dimensions 12 cm and 8 cm overlap to form the shape below. Equal lengths are shown on the shape.

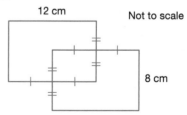

What is the perimeter of the shape?

A 60 cm
B 48 cm
C 66 cm
D 72 cm
E 68 cm

30 Letters of the alphabet are written using straight or curved lines. Here are six letters:

E F H L T Z

Two letters are chosen at random. What is the highest possible total number of right angles in the chosen letters?

3	4	6	8	9
A	B	C	D	E

31 The grid shows the location of four points of interest.

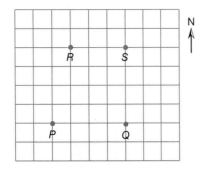

Tim left *P* and walked 8 km to *Q*. He then walked north to *S* and west to *R*. What is the total distance he walked from *P* to *R*?

A 24 km
B 5 km
C 26 km
D 10 km
E 22 km

32 At a football match, Jamie and Kate sell programs. They both sell eight programs every minute. How many programs do they sell in a quarter of an hour?

60	120	180	240	480
A	B	C	D	E

33 This is a square prism.

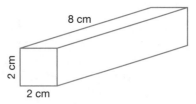

What is the total length of all the edges?
A 20 cm
B 24 cm
C 32 cm
D 48 cm
E 54 cm

34 A survey of students was conducted to find their favourite sports. The pictograph is used to display the results.

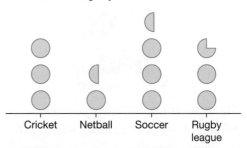

Twelve students said their favourite sport was cricket. How many more students like soccer than those who prefer netball?

2	3	6	8	10
A	B	C	D	E

35 What is the total number of unseen dots on these normal dice?

7	13	21	25	29
A	B	C	D	E

SAMPLE TEST 6

1 If each of these numbers is rounded to the nearest hundred, which number changes the most?

A 76
B 119
C 245
D 378
E 483

2 The product of what number and 8 equals 160?

152	168	2	20	1040
A	B	C	D	E

3 To celebrate his birthday, Jack and four of his friends went out for dinner. The total cost of the meal was $220. The four friends decided to split the bill evenly so Jack paid nothing. How much did each friend pay?

A $44
B $45
C $54
D $55
E $60

4 How many whole numbers between 110 and 150 are multiples of 3?

11	15	12	14	13
A	B	C	D	E

5 A quarter of a number is 12. What is twice the number?

6	8	24	48	96
A	B	C	D	E

6 The shape is formed using 12 identical squares. Two-thirds of the squares are shaded.

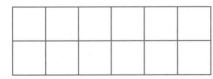

How many squares remain unshaded?

3	2	6	8	4
A	B	C	D	E

7 In the Mt Gambier scouts troop there are 27 boys and girls. There are three more boys than girls.
How many girls are in the troop?

10	12	15	24	13
A	B	C	D	E

8 A market stallholder sells pot plants.
For every three wattles sold, the stallholder sells two rose plants.
How many rose plants were sold by the stallholder if 12 wattles were sold?

5	6	8	9	10
A	B	C	D	E

9 Lucas is allowed 45 minutes of personal screen time on Sunday nights. If the time starts at 7:25, what time will it finish?

A 8:00
B 8:05
C 8:10
D 8:15
E 8:20

10 Which of these letters has the greatest number of lines of symmetry?

M	D	E	I	Z
A	B	C	D	E

11 Here is a number line.

Which letter represents the fraction $\frac{3}{4}$?

A	B	C	D	E
A	B	C	D	E

12 Simone starts with a piece of paper in the shape of a triangle, as shown.

She makes **one fold** in the paper, without moving it in any other way.
Which of the following shapes could **not** be the result?

A

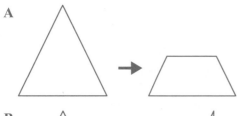

B

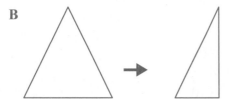

C

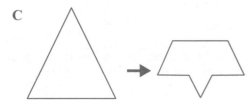

D

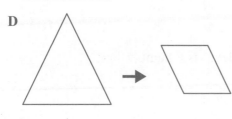

E

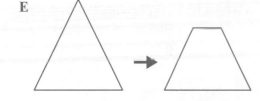

13 If each small square in the grid covers 2 cm², what is the size of the shaded area?

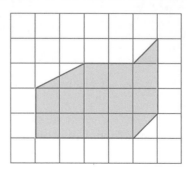

A 27 cm²
B 28 cm²
C 29 cm²
D 30 cm²
E 31 cm²

14 The diagram shows six circles arranged in a triangle. The numbers 1 to 6 are written in the circles so that the sums of the three numbers on each side of the triangle are the same.

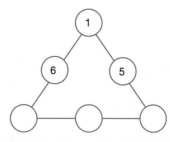

When the puzzle is solved, what will be the total of each side?

8	9	10	11	12
A	B	C	D	E

15 Here is a pattern of numbers.

4, 12, 6, 18, 9 …

What is the seventh number in the pattern?

36	$4\frac{1}{2}$	24	27	$13\frac{1}{2}$
A	B	C	D	E

16 Here is a number chart. Denise shades the multiples of 4.

1	2	3	4	5	6	7	8	9	10
11	12	13	14	15	16	17	18	19	20
21	22	23	24	25	26	27	28	29	30

Here is another section of the chart.

151	152	153	154	155	156	157	158	159	160
161	162	163	164	165	166	167	168	169	170

If Denise continues in the same number pattern, how many squares will she shade in this section of the chart?

5	6	7	8	10
A	B	C	D	E

17 A circuit in the shape of a rectangle is set up on the school oval. The rectangle has a length of 80 m and a width of 50 m. Symon runs around the circuit four times. What is the distance he has run?

A 520 m
B 1040 m
C 800 m
D 260 m
E 940 m

18 Ingrid thinks of a number, adds 8 and then subtracts 7. She then adds another 10. If she ends up with 18, what number did she start with?

8	4	5	6	7
A	B	C	D	E

19 In this number sentence, ▲ represents a missing number.

$$10 \times 36 = 5 \times \blacktriangle \times 9$$

What is the value of ▲?

16	12	4	6	8
A	B	C	D	E

20 The shape is formed by joining 10 identical squares.

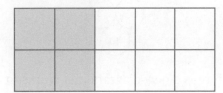

The area of the shaded section is 12 cm². What is the area of the unshaded section?

A 12 cm²
B 14 cm²
C 15 cm²
D 16 cm²
E 18 cm²

21 Mila fills and then empties a 300-mL bottle of water into an empty 6-L container. It takes half a minute to fill and then pour the water into the container. How long will it take Mila to fill the container?

A 6 minutes
B 8 minutes
C 10 minutes
D 12 minutes
E 20 minutes

22 The diagram below shows a pan balance.

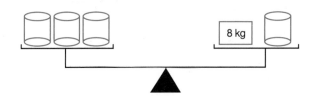

What is the total mass of the four identical cylinders?

A 8 kg
B 32 kg
C 16 kg
D 24 kg
E 18 kg

23 In this diagram, 7 + 3 = 10.

Here is a new diagram that works in the same way.

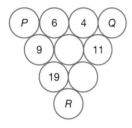

What is the sum of *P*, *Q* and *R*?

52	56	48	58	50
A	**B**	**C**	**D**	**E**

24 The diagram shows two identical circles that fit inside a rectangle. The radius of each circle is 3 cm.

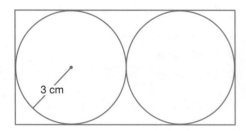

What is the area of the rectangle?
A 54 cm²
B 60 cm²
C 64 cm²
D 72 cm²
E 84 cm²

25 An unopened jar of strawberry jam has a mass of 320 g. When it is half full, the mass is 200 g. What is the mass of the empty jar?

A 40 g   B 90 g   C 50 g
D 60 g   E 80 g

26 Logan was born on 15 May and his cousin Ella was born five weeks later. Which of these is Ella's birthday?
A 15 June
B 16 June
C 17 June
D 18 June
E 19 June

27 The graph shows the number of supporters of five football teams.

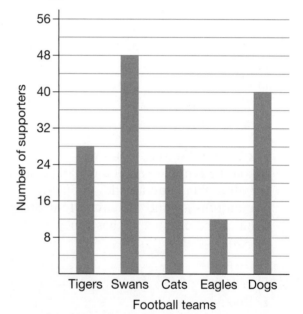

Here are three statements about the graph:
1 There are four times as many Swans supporters as Eagles supporters.
2 There are twice as many Dogs supporters as Cats supporters.
3 One hundred people support the Tigers, Swans or Cats.

Using the information on the graph, which of the statements is/are correct?
A statement 1 only
B statement 2 only
C statement 3 only
D statements 1 and 2 only
E statements 1 and 3 only

28 Letters are written on a square grid. The square is folded along the dotted line to form a rectangle. The rectangle is then folded along the dotted line to form a square.

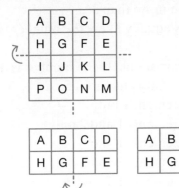

Which of these letters is behind the letter G?

E	O	H	M	K
A	**B**	**C**	**D**	**E**

29 The grid shows the location of seven trees in a park.

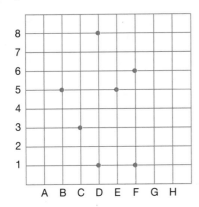

The distance between the trees at B5 and E5 is 24 m. What is the distance between the trees at D1 and D8?

A 80 km

B 7 m

C 64 m

D 8 m

E 56 m

30 How many right angles are in this design?

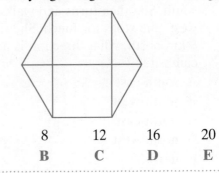

4	8	12	16	20
A	**B**	**C**	**D**	**E**

31 The frame of a cube is made using wire. Each edge is 4 cm. What is the total length of wire used?

A 24 cm

B 60 cm

C 28 cm

D 36 cm

E 48 cm

32 The graphs below show the number of coloured balls in two bags.

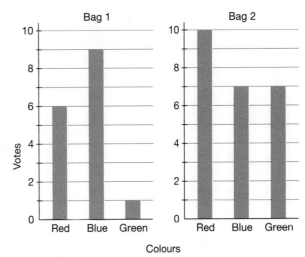

Elijah removes balls from each bag and places them in the other bag so that the bags are identical.
What is the total number of balls moved by Elijah?

3	4	5	6	7
A	**B**	**C**	**D**	**E**

33 Emma leaves her campsite and walks 4 km south. She then turns and walks 4 km west. She stops for lunch. She then walks 8 km north. What direction is her campsite?

A south-east

B south-west

C north-east

D north-west

E north

34 In a code, each letter is represented by a **different** whole number **greater than 1**. Words are replaced by the product of their letters.

For example, if M = 6 and E = 4, then ME = 6 × 4 = 24.

If MOO = 20 and ZOO = 12, what is the value of ZOOM?

A 36

B 44

C 48

D 60

E 72

35 The faces of a cube are numbered 1 to 6. The cube is rolled and the number that is face up is recorded.

Which of these statements is/are correct?

1 It is less likely the number is less than 3 than more than 3.

2 It is equally likely the number is a 3 or a 6.

3 It is more likely the number is a factor of 4 than a factor of 5.

A statement 1 only

B statements 1 and 2 only

C statements 1 and 3 only

D statements 2 and 3 only

E statements 1, 2 and 3

OPPORTUNITY CLASS—STYLE TEST | **Mathematical Reasoning**

SAMPLE TEST 7

1 When Bonnie divides 39 by her favourite number, the remainder is 4. Which of these could be Bonnie's favourite number?

3	4	5	6	9
A	B	C	D	E

2 The shape below is made from eight small identical rectangles. Two of the rectangles are shaded.

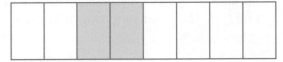

How many more rectangles need to be shaded so that three-quarters of the shape is shaded?

1	2	4	5	6
A	B	C	D	E

3 The total of Joseph's age and Ethan's age is 20. If Ethan was 6 when Joseph was born, how old will Joseph be in 2 years?

5	6	7	8	9
A	B	C	D	E

4 The thermometer shows the temperature at 6 am and 2 pm yesterday.

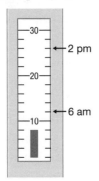

How much did the temperature rise?

A 7 degrees

B 9 degrees

C 14 degrees

D 16 degrees

E 18 degrees

5 What is the square of the sum of six and four?

36	40	100	52	16
A	B	C	D	E

6 Kai rounds the number 349 342 to the nearest hundred. What is the new number?

340	350	349 300	349 340	349 400
A	B	C	D	E

7 In this diagram, 5 + 3 = 8.

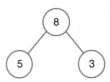

Here is a new diagram that works in the same way.

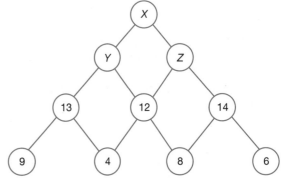

What is the value of *X*?

25	41	71	36	51
A	B	C	D	E

8 Mo's birthday is 3 weeks after Charlie's birthday. If Mo was born on 2 September, what day is Charlie's birthday?

A 19 August

B 10 August

C 13 August

D 12 August

E 11 August

9 Owen bought 6 kg of carrots. He paid for the carrots with a $20 note and received four $2 coins in change. What did Oliver pay when he bought 2 kg of carrots?

$3	$4	$4.50	$5	$6
A	B	C	D	E

10 Which of these is **not** a factor of 84?

4	8	12	21	42
A	B	C	D	E

11

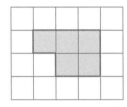

What fraction of the grid is shaded?

$\frac{1}{2}$	$\frac{1}{10}$	$\frac{1}{5}$	$\frac{1}{3}$	$\frac{1}{4}$
A	B	C	D	E

12 The diagram shows six circles arranged in a triangle. The numbers 1 to 6 are written in the circles so that the sums of the three numbers on each side of the triangle are the same.

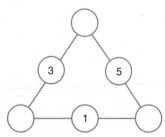

When the puzzle is solved, what will be the total of each side?

8	9	10	11	12
A	B	C	D	E

13 Here is a pattern of numbers

2181, 3273, 4365, 5457 …

What is the next number in the pattern?

A 6649   B 6549   C 6538

D 6659   E 6648

14 Yesterday morning Greg completed 12 push-ups. He plans to increase the number by two every morning. How many push-ups does Greg plan to complete 5 days from now?

20	22	23	24	25
A	B	C	D	E

15 Students were surveyed to find the number of books they read in the school holidays. The results are shown in the graph below.

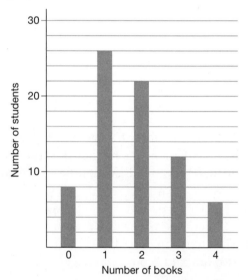

Scott reads the graph and makes three claims:

1 Seven more students read one book than the number of students who read three books.

2 Forty students read at least two books.

3 Twice as many students read three books as the number who read four books.

Using the information on the graph, which of Scott's claims is/are correct?

A claim 1 only

B claim 2 only

C claim 3 only

D claims 2 and 3 only

E claims 1, 2 and 3

16 Which digit has been replaced with ▲ in this number sentence?

$$359 - 1\blacktriangle 6 = 183$$

3	4	5	6	7
A	B	C	D	E

17 A rectangle is drawn inside a square on the grid below. The area of the rectangle is 16 cm². What is the size of the shaded area?

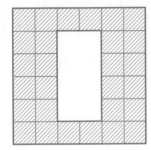

A 52 cm²

B 48 cm²

C 60 cm²

D 64 cm²

E 56 cm²

18 Here are five spinners.

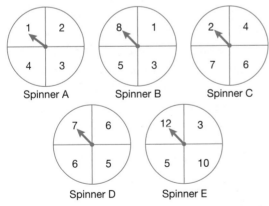

The arrow is spun on each spinner. Which spinner has the greatest chance of landing on an even number?

A   B   C   D   E

19 Hermann thought of a number. He added 8, multiplied by 4, subtracted 6 and divided by 2. The result was 21. What was Hermann's original number?

2	3	4	6	8
A	B	C	D	E

20 Imogen has two containers which can hold 500 mL each. Container A has 120 mL of water and container B has 165 mL of water. Imogen pours half of the water from container A into container B. How much more water does she need to completely fill container B?

A 335 mL

B 275 mL

C 345 mL

D 225 mL

E 215 mL

21 A rectangle is formed using four identical squares. The perimeter of the rectangle is 30 cm.

What is the area of each of the squares?

A 12 cm²

B 3 cm²

C 6 cm²

D 10 cm²

E 9 cm²

22 Two-thirds of the mass of an object is 24 kg. What is the total mass?

A 16 kg

B 18 kg

C 28 kg

D 32 kg

E 36 kg

23 Henry has a bedside clock that loses 2 minutes every hour. When he goes to bed at 9:00 pm, he makes sure the clock is accurate. When he wakes the next morning at 6:30 am, what time will be showing on his clock?

A 6:10

B 6:11

C 6:12

D 6:19

E 6:21

24 How many of these shapes have at least two lines of symmetry?

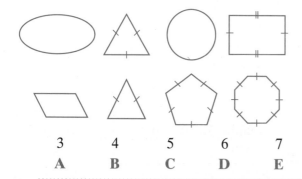

3	4	5	6	7
A	B	C	D	E

25 There were 24 chocolates in a box. Adam ate one-quarter of the chocolates on Saturday. He ate one-third of the remaining chocolates on Sunday. How many chocolates were left in the box?

7	17	18	12	6
A	B	C	D	E

26 How many right angles are in this design?

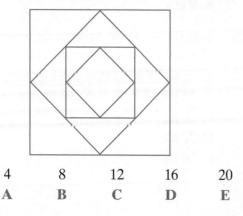

4	8	12	16	20
A	B	C	D	E

27 Letters are written on a square grid. The square is folded along the dotted line to form a rectangle. The rectangle is then folded along the dotted line to form a square.

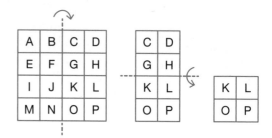

Which of these letters is behind the letter P?

A	B	E	I	N
A	B	C	D	E

28 A plane flies between two cities. If it takes off at 10:45 pm and lands at 7:10 am, how long was the flight?

A 7 hours 25 minutes

B 7 hours 35 minutes

C 8 hours 25 minutes

D 8 hours 35 minutes

E 8 hours 25 minutes

29 In a park, an oak tree is 76 m west of a pine tree. The pine tree is 19 m east of a gum tree. Rocky the dog walks from the gum tree to the oak tree. How far does Rocky walk?

A 55 m

B 57 m

C 95 m

D 97 m

E 114 m

30 The dimensions of a rectangular prism are 5 cm by 4 cm by 3 cm. What is the total length of the edges of the prism?

A 12 cm   B 24 cm   C 48 cm

D 60 cm   E 96 cm

31 Kara starts with a piece of paper in the shape of the letter L, as shown.

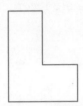

She makes **one fold** in the paper, without moving it in any other way.
Which of the following shapes could **not** be the result?

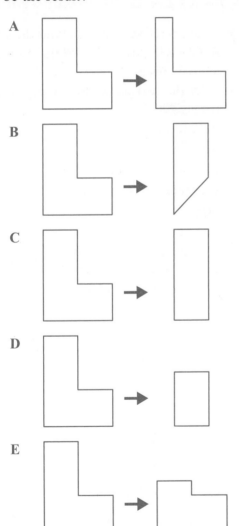

A

B

C

D

E

32 The dimensions of a photo are 15 cm by 10 cm.

The photo is enlarged so that the perimeter is 100 cm. What is the area of the enlargement?
A 150 cm^2
B 300 cm^2
C 450 cm^2
D 600 cm^2
E 1200 cm^2

33 Elsie is standing at the position marked as *X* on the grid.

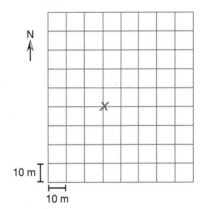

She walks in the following directions, one after the other:
1. 20 m south
2. 40 m east
3. 50 m north
4. 40 m west
When she is finished, how far is Elsie from her starting position?
A 20 m   B 0 m   C 4 m
D 40 m   E 30 m

34 This shape is made from five small, identical cubes.

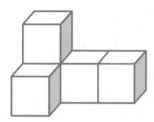

The shape is picked up and viewed from all directions.

How many cube faces **cannot** be seen?

4	5	6	7	8
A	B	C	D	E

35 Students in classes 4P and 5K voted in student elections. The votes for Aria, Levi, Jack and Isla are recorded in the graphs below.

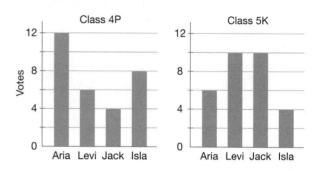

Here are three statements about the graphs:

1 In Class 4P Aria received three times as many votes as Isla.

2 Over the two classes Levi received 16 votes.

3 Aria received the most votes from the two classes.

Using the information on the graphs, which of the statements is/are correct?

A statement 1 only

B statement 2 only

C statements 1 and 2 only

D statements 2 and 3 only

E statements 1, 2 and 3

SAMPLE TEST 8

1 Here is a café menu:

MENU

Coffee	Regular	$4.50
	Large	$5.00
Hot chocolate	Regular	$5.00
	Large	$5.50
Soft drink		$4.20
Slice		$5.50
Banana bread		$4.80
Muffin		$5.20

Frida ordered two large coffees, a regular hot chocolate, a banana bread and a muffin. What was the total cost?

A $25.00
B $24.20
C $24.00
D $24.60
E $25.20

2 Here are four identical squares:

The squares are joined.

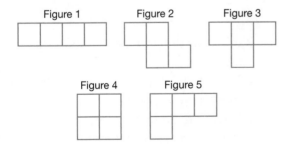

Figure 1   Figure 2   Figure 3

Figure 4   Figure 5

Which figure has the smallest perimeter?
A Figure 1
B Figure 2
C Figure 3
D Figure 4
E Figure 5

3 In a restaurant there are 6 tables. Each table has 4 legs. Twice as many tables can seat 8 customers as those that can seat 4 customers. If each chair has 4 legs, what is the total number of legs of the tables and chairs in the restaurant?

| 40 | 46 | 144 | 160 | 184 |
| A | B | C | D | E |

4 Eve visits the dentist on Thursday 28 July for a check-up. Afterwards, she makes another appointment for 11 days later. On what day is her next appointment?
A Monday 8 August
B Monday 9 August
C Tuesday 8 August
D Tuesday 9 August
E Tuesday 10 August

5 How many lines of symmetry has this shape?

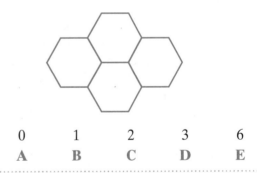

| 0 | 1 | 2 | 3 | 6 |
| A | B | C | D | E |

6 This sign is in the front window of a bakery.

Buy 4 bread rolls
Receive a 5th bread roll
FREE

Simone pays for 14 bread rolls. How many will she receive?

| 15 | 16 | 17 | 18 | 19 |
| A | B | C | D | E |

7 Jason thinks of four different whole numbers that multiply together to give 48. Which of these could be two of the numbers?

A 1 and 18
B 1 and 24
C 2 and 24
D 4 and 7
E 4 and 6

8 James has two fences of the same size to paint. He spent a day painting one-third of one of the fences. How many **more** days will he take to finish both fences?

2	3	5	6	8
A	B	C	D	E

9 Three numbers have the same sum and product. What is the sum if each of the three numbers is doubled?

6	8	12	16	20
A	B	C	D	E

10 Hannah located the numbers 9 and 24 on a number line. She worked out the distance between the two numbers. Which of these pairs of numbers are the same distance apart as 9 and 24?

A 8 and 22
B 12 and 25
C 16 and 32
D 39 and 64
E 50 and 65

11 Robbie was given money from his relatives for his birthday. He used half the money to buy a console game for $30 and a pair of shoes for $60. Which number sentence can be used to find the amount of money in dollars he was given for his birthday?

A $30 \div 2 + 60 \div 2$
B $30 + 60 \div 2$
C $30 + 60 \times 2$
D $30 \div 2 + 60$
E $30 \times 2 + 60 \times 2$

12 Henry wrote a list of all the even numbers from 20 to 40. He then circled the numbers that are multiples of 4. How many numbers are **not** circled?

6	2	4	3	5
A	B	C	D	E

13 The shape consists of 10 identical squares.

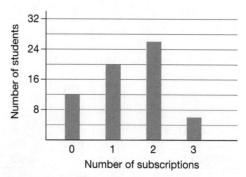

Stacey shades two of the squares. Matthew shades three-quarters of the remaining squares. How many squares remain unshaded?

2	3	4	5	6
A	B	C	D	E

14 A group of people were surveyed to find the number of streaming subscriptions they have purchased. The results are shown in the graph below.

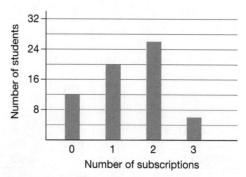

Rani reads the graph and makes three claims:

1 More than 30 people have more than one streaming service.

2 There are 20 more people with two streaming services than the number with three streaming services.

3 Sixty people were surveyed.

Using the information on the graph, which of Rani's claims is/are correct?

A claim 1 only   B claim 2 only
C claims 1 and 2 only
D claims 2 and 3 only
E claims 1, 2 and 3

15 The total number of faces on three solids is 17. One solid is a hexagonal prism and another is a square-based pyramid. What is the other solid?

A cube

B pentagonal prism

C pentagonal pyramid

D hexagonal pyramid

E triangular pyramid

16 A group of 16 students were surveyed to find how they spent their weekend.

- Ten students went to the beach.
- Eight students went to the movies.
- Three students did not go to the beach or the movies.

How many students went to the beach and the movies?

4	5	6	7	8
A	B	C	D	E

17 The number in each of the squares is the result of adding the numbers in the nearest circles.

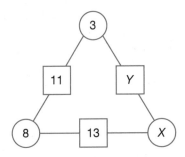

For example, on the left side, 3 + 8 = 11. What is the value of X multiplied by Y?

12	25	30	40	32
A	B	C	D	E

18 A sequence of figures is shown on the grid below.

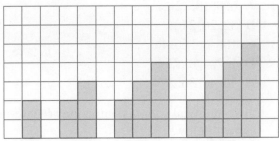

Figure 1 Figure 2 Figure 3 Figure 4

The sequence continues. What would be the area of figure 6?

A 19 square units

B 24 square units

C 25 square units

D 26 square units

E 27 square units

19 What number must be placed in the box to make a true number sentence?

$$148 - \boxed{} = 25 + 25$$

98	102	88	112	127
A	B	C	D	E

20 In this magic square, numbers in each row, column and diagonal add to the same number.

	2	*	13
5			8
9	7		12
	14	15	1

What is the value of *?

16	2	5	3	10
A	B	C	D	E

21 Which of these sequences does not have 16 as one of its numbers?
A 6, 8, 10, 12 …
B 32, 28, 24 …
C 106, 86, 66, 46 …
D 1, 2, 4, 8 …
E 56, 46, 36, 26 …

22 Two identical squares with sides 6 cm are shown below.

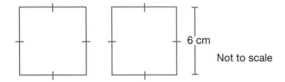

6 cm
Not to scale

The squares are moved so that a part of the squares overlap.

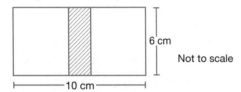

6 cm
Not to scale
10 cm

What is the area of the shaded overlap?

12 cm²	8 cm²	6 cm²	18 cm²	4 cm²
A	**B**	**C**	**D**	**E**

23 The diagram shows two containers. Juice has been poured into both containers.

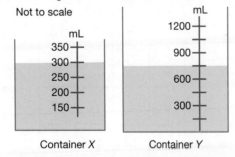

Not to scale

mL
350
300
250
200
150
Container X

mL
1200
900
600
300
Container Y

Half the juice from container X is poured into container Y. How much juice is now in container Y?
A 900 mL   **B** 750 mL   **C** 700 mL
D 600 mL   **E** 1000 mL

24 Prawns are priced at $36 per kilogram. How much will Alma pay for 1 kg 500 g of prawns?
A $54   **B** $41   **C** $86
D $52   **E** $60

25 In 2022 Margot turned 57. In what year was Margot born?
A 1957
B 1962
C 1963
D 1975
E 1965

26 An electrician arrived at Stella's apartment at 10:26 am and left at 11:12 am. How long was the electrician at the apartment?
A 56 minutes
B 48 minutes
C 52 minutes
D 96 minutes
E 46 minutes

27 One corner of a 6 cm by 6 cm square is removed. The removed section is a 2 cm by 2 cm square.

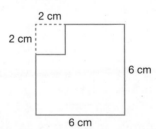

2 cm
2 cm
6 cm
6 cm

The other three corners of the large square are also removed using 2 cm by 2 cm squares. What is the perimeter of the new shape?
A 12 cm
B 14 cm
C 16 cm
D 18 cm
E 24 cm

28 Silas starts with a piece of paper in the shape of a trapezium, as shown.

He makes **one fold** in the paper, without moving it in any other way.
Which of the following shapes could **not** be the result?

A
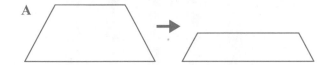

B
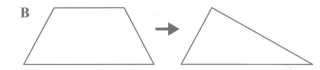

C
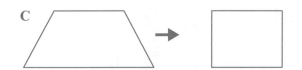

D
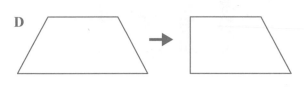

E
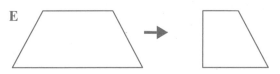

29 Mo looked at a rectangular prism and a triangular prism. What is the total number of edges on the two prisms?

16	18	20	21	24
A	B	C	D	E

30 Amelia is shading squares on the grid.

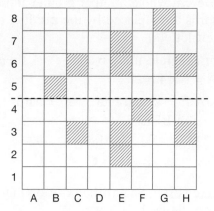

She wants the horizontal dotted line to be a line of symmetry where each square on the top reflects to a square on the bottom. She needs to shade three more squares. Which squares should Amelia shade?

A B2, F6, G2
B B2, F5, G1
C B4, F6, G8
D B4, F5, G8
E B4, F5, G1

31 How many acute angles are in this design?

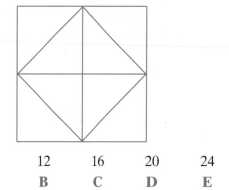

8	12	16	20	24
A	B	C	D	E

32 Adam has counted the toy cars in his collection. He arranges the cars into 7 groups of 13 cars and has an even number of cars left over. Which of these **could** be the total number of cars in Adam's collection?

87	94	96	97	98
A	B	C	D	E

33 In a code, each letter is represented by a **different** whole number **greater than 1**. Words are replaced by the product of their letters.

For example, if P = 6 and A = 4, then PA = 6 × 4 = 24.

If BEE = 45 and FEE = 36, what is the value of BEEF?

72	90	180	192	216
A	**B**	**C**	**D**	**E**

34 Luke is standing at the position marked as *P* on the grid.

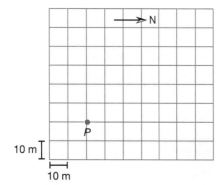

He walks in the following directions, one after the other:

1. 40 m north
2. 30 m west
3. 20 m south
4. 10 m east
5. 20 m south

When he is finished, how far is Luke from his starting position?

A 0 m
B 4 m
C 20 m
D 40 m
E 150 m

35 Gianna drives a taxi on weekdays. The two graphs below show the number of hours Gianna worked in two weeks. She has not recorded the number of hours she worked on Friday in Week 2.

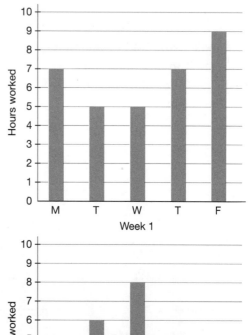

Week 1

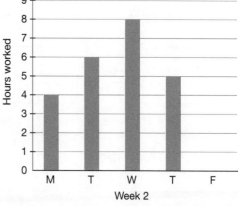

Week 2

Gianna worked the same number of hours in both weeks. How many hours did Gianna work on Friday in week 2?

A 8 hours
B 9 hours
C 10 hours
D 6 hours
E 7 hours

SAMPLE TEST 9

40 MIN

1 Which number is halfway between 14 and 84?

54	44	48	34	49
A	B	C	D	E

2 Max thinks of a number. He adds 5 and doubles the result. When he subtracts 4, his answer is 12. What was Max's original number?

21	11	6	3	13
A	B	C	D	E

3 What is the total of two hundred and forty, fifty-three and two?

243	242	292	295	2932
A	B	C	D	E

4 Emma buys a pair of soccer boots. She pays $100 and receives $27 in change. Her friend Zoe also buys a pair of boots and pays $12 more than Emma. How much did Zoe pay for her boots?

$35	$61	$65	$75	$85
A	B	C	D	E

5 Which of these solids has more than two triangular faces?

A triangular prism

B square prism

C hexagonal prism

D square pyramid

E cone

6 A download is scheduled to take 2 minutes 14 seconds. After 75 seconds, what time remains for the download to complete?

A 63 seconds

B 59 seconds

C 69 seconds

D 71 seconds

E 79 seconds

7 Elaine has drawn these five designs.

Design 1   Design 2

Design 3

Design 4   Design 5

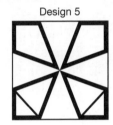

Which design has MORE than one line of symmetry?

A Design 1

B Design 2

C Design 3

D Design 4

E Design 5

8 Jade has 30 cards numbered 1 to 30. How many of the cards are **not** multiples of 4?

17	21	23	24	27
A	B	C	D	E

9 The students in a small school vote to elect a school captain. Olivia receives 40 votes, which is 10 more than Noah. Liam gets half as many votes as Olivia and Elijah gets twice as many as Noah. Amelia gets the smallest number of votes. Which of these could be the total number of votes?

140	160	172	178	180
A	B	C	D	E

10 Kristie is standing at the position marked *A* on the grid.

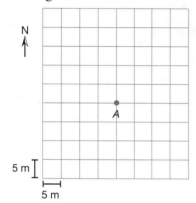

She walks in the following directions, one after the other:

1. 20 m west
2. 25 m north
3. 30 m east
4. 40 m south
5. 10 m west

Kristie finishes at *B*. What is the distance and direction of *B* from *A*?

A   *B* is 30 m south of *A*.

B   *B* is 15 m south of *A*.

C   *B* is 10 m west of *A*.

D   *B* is 15 m west of *A*.

E   *B* is 20 m west of *A*.

11 The diagram shows two empty cubes without lids. The cubes hold 8 L and 64 L of water.

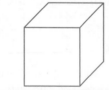

Jacinta fills the small cube with water and pours the water into the large cube. She wants to half fill the large cube with water. How many **more** small cubes of water does she need?

4	7	8	12	3
A	B	C	D	E

12 There are 20 parking spaces in a car park. If three-fifths of the spaces are being used, how many are vacant?

8	10	12	14	15
A	B	C	D	E

13 Here is a diagram with seven circles arranged in columns and rows. The numbers 1 to 7 are written in the circles so that the sum of the three numbers in each line is 12.

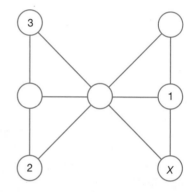

Which number replaces the letter *X*?

3	5	2	1	6
A	B	C	D	E

14 What number must be placed in the box to make a true number sentence?

$$6 \times \boxed{} - 12 = 48$$

4	6	9	10	12
A	B	C	D	E

15 Ana places a set of cards face down on a table. She turns over three-tenths of the cards. If 21 cards are still face down, how many cards are in the set?

24	30	33	36	70
A	B	C	D	E

16 Tom has a mass of 46 kg. His younger sister Emma is 7 kg lighter. His older brother is 5 kg heavier. What is the total mass of the three siblings?

A   58 kg   B   134 kg   C   135 kg

D   136 kg   E   174 kg

17 On Sebastian's 12th birthday, his father was 38 years old. If Sebastian was 15 in 2021, in what year was his father born?

A 1980

B 1981

C 1982

D 1983

E 1984

18 What number would replace the * in the table?

4	10	7	9	2
7	25	16	*	1

18	20	21	22	23
A	B	C	D	E

19 Stella is driving her car on a straight and level section of road. She travels 3600 m in 3 minutes. At this speed, how far will she travel in 20 seconds?

A 500 m

B 300 m

C 450 m

D 540 m

E 400 m

20 A 36-cm length of wire is cut into two pieces. Both pieces are bent into squares. The larger square has a perimeter of 20 cm. What is the length of each side of the smaller square?

A 6 cm

B 4 cm

C 8 cm

D 5 cm

E 2 cm

21 Mitchell leaves home at 6:15 am. He takes 15 minutes to ride to his fitness centre. He spends 20 minutes in the pool and 25 minutes in the gym. Mitchell then rides home, arriving at 7:40 am.

How long did he take to ride home?

A 20 minutes

B 10 minutes

C 15 minutes

D 30 minutes

E 25 minutes

22 A rectangle is formed from identical squares. Some of the squares are shaded.

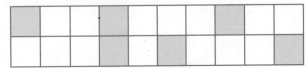

How many more squares need to be shaded so that three-quarters of the rectangle is shaded?

8	7	10	11	9
A	B	C	D	E

23 The school principal needs to randomly choose students to complete a survey. She uses an alphabetical list of 100 student names. She chooses the seventh student and then every fifth student after that. How many students are chosen?

12	15	19	20	21
A	B	C	D	E

24 Janice is using cans to make a series of towers.

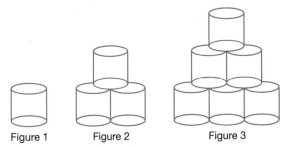

Figure 1   Figure 2   Figure 3

The first figure has one can, the second figure has three cans, and so on. Which figure will be made using 78 cans?

9	10	11	12	13
A	B	C	D	E

25 In this diagram, 2 × 4 = 8.

Here is a new diagram that works in the same way:

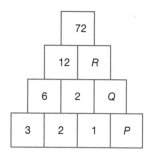

What is the sum of *P* and *R*?

6	9	12	8	2
A	B	C	D	E

26 Myles draws a rectangle 5 cm long and 4 cm wide.

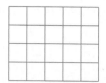

He has a small paper rectangle which is 3 cm long and 1 cm wide. He wants to make a new shape by placing the small rectangle in one of four positions shown as *W*, *X*, *Y* or *Z*.

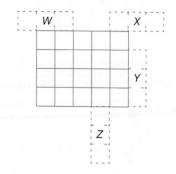

Myles wants the perimeter of the new shape to be 6 cm more than the perimeter of his original rectangle. Which of these positions are possible?

A *X* only
B *Y* and *Z* only
C *X* and *Z* only
D *X*, *Y* and *Z* only
E *W*, *X*, *Y* and *Z*

27 The ten digits 0 to 9 are written in digital form using only vertical and horizontal lines.

How many right angles are used in writing the odd digits?

13	7	12	16	15
A	B	C	D	E

28 Andrew is shading squares on the grid.

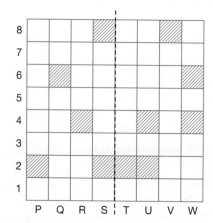

He wants the vertical dotted line to be a line of symmetry where each square on the left reflects to a square on the right. How many more squares should Andrew shade?

1	2	4	6	7
A	B	C	D	E

SAMPLE TEST 9

29 $16 \times 45 = 2 \times \triangle \times 5$

What is the missing number $\triangle$?

30	36	40	72	80
A	B	C	D	E

30 Agnes counts from 3 to 8 in jumps of $\frac{1}{3}$.

Pablo counts from 7 to 15 in jumps of $\frac{1}{2}$.

Which statement is correct?

A Agnes makes 3 more jumps than Pablo.

B Agnes makes 1 more jump than Pablo.

B They make the same number of jumps.

D Pablo makes 1 more jump than Agnes.

E Pablo makes 3 more jumps than Agnes.

31 Brodie has a bag containing five counters numbered 1 to 5. Shane has a bag containing 10 counters numbered 6 to 15. Each boy randomly chooses a counter from his own bag.

Which of these statements is/are correct?

1 Brodie has a greater chance of selecting an even number than an odd number.

2 Shane has a greater chance than Brodie of selecting a number between 4 and 8.

3 Brodie has a lower chance than Shane of selecting a multiple of 5.

A none

B statement 2 only

C statement 3 only

D statements 2 and 3 only

E statements 1, 2 and 3

32 The graph shows the ages of school representatives at a regional athletics carnival.

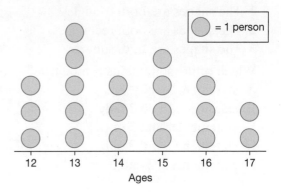

A student made these claims about the information in the graph.

1 Eight students were aged 12 or 13.

2 There were more students aged 13 or 14 than aged 16 or 17.

3 Twenty students represented the school.

Using the information on the graph, which of the student's claims is/are correct?

A claim 1 only

B claim 2 only

C claims 1 and 2 only

D claims 1 and 3 only

E claims 1, 2 and 3

33 Here is a net of a cube.

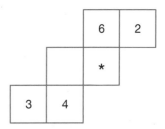

The net is folded to form a cube. Numbers on opposite faces multiply to the same number. What is the number represented by the *?

5	8	12	1	6
A	B	C	D	E

34 Sam has a square piece of paper. He cuts the paper into two equal shapes. Sam makes these three statements.

1 The shapes are both triangles.
2 The shapes are both rectangles.
3 The shapes are both squares.

Which of the statements can be true?
A statement 3 only
B statement 1 and 2 only
C statement 1 and 3 only
D statement 2 and 3 only
E statements 1, 2 and 3

35 The column graph shows the number of laps Joe ran in a week. Each lap is 3 km in length.

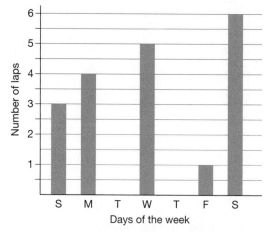

Anish reads the graph and makes three claims:

1 Joe completed 12 laps in the first four days of the week.
2 On five days Joe ran at least two laps.
3 Joe ran more than 60 km in the week.

Using the information on the graph, which of Anish's claims is/are correct?
A claims 1, 2 and 3
B claims 2 and 3 only
C claims 1 and 2 only
D claim 1 only
E claim 2 only

SAMPLE TEST 10

1 George picked 94 oranges from his backyard tree. He gave his friends 10 oranges each and had 34 left over. How many of George's friends were given oranges?

5	6	7	8	9
A	B	C	D	E

2 A shape is formed using four identical squares.

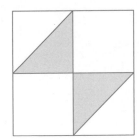

What fraction of the shape is shaded?

$\frac{1}{4}$	$\frac{1}{6}$	$\frac{1}{5}$	$\frac{1}{8}$	$\frac{1}{10}$
A	B	C	D	E

3 For their school photo, students in class 4K are arranged according to their height. Jack is the tallest and Mikayla is the shortest. Lachie is tenth in line. There are 14 students between Lachie and Mikayla. How many students are in the line?

24	25	26	27	28
A	B	C	D	E

4 A piece of wire 20 cm long is bent into a rectangle. The width of the rectangle is 4 cm. What is the length of the rectangle?

A 8 cm   **B** 10 cm   **C** 6 cm
D 4 cm   **E** 5 cm

5 What is the value of *X* on the number line?

2140   2260   X

A 2280
B 2300
C 2320
D 2340
E 2360

6 Two numbers add to 100. One of the numbers is 56 more than the other. What is the smaller number?

44	33	22	28	32
A	B	C	D	E

7 Sam can buy 36 mangos for $27. How much will she pay for 48 mangos?

$36	$32	$38	$39	$45
A	B	C	D	E

8 Caiaphas is thinking of a number. When he divides it by 2 there is a remainder of 1. When he divides it by 3 there is a remainder of 2. If the number has digits that add to 8, what is the number?

23	26	35	44	62
A	B	C	D	E

9 At 1 pm a baker has 12 pies for sale. By 3 pm she has sold three-quarters of the pies. How many pies remain?

6	1	2	4	3
A	B	C	D	E

10 Neil gave his two brothers, John and Jack, money to be given to their children. John has three children and each was given $1200. Jack was given half as much as John. If Jack has four children, how much will each of Jack's children receive?

A $400   **B** $450   **C** $500
D $540   **E** $600

11 The diagram shows six circles arranged in a triangle. The numbers 1 to 6 are written in the circles so that the sums of the three numbers on each side of the triangle are the same.

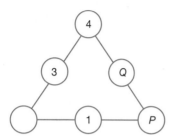

When the puzzle is solved, what will be the quotient of *P* and *Q*?

1	2	3	4	6
A	**B**	**C**	**D**	**E**

12 Which of these number sentences can be used to find half a number, if three-quarters of the number is 12?

A $12 \div 3 \times 2$
B $12 \div 3 + 2$
C $12 \times 3 \div 2$
D $12 \times 2 + 3$
E $12 \times 3 - 6 \times 3$

13 Olivia draws a square on a grid with side length 4 cm. She has used the letters *P*, *Q*, *R* and *S* to label four of the small squares in the grid.

P			
	Q		
			S
	R		

Olivia wants to cut out and remove one small square. Which square should be removed to increase the perimeter by 2 cm?

A *P* only   B *Q* only
C *P* or *Q* only   D *P*, *R* or *S* only
E *R* or *S* only

14 In this diagram, 7 + 5 = 12.

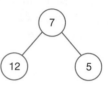

Here is a new diagram that works in the same way:

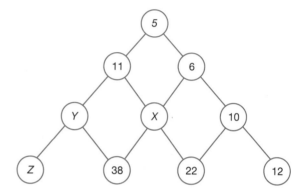

What is the value of *Z*?

73	91	77	81	65
A	**B**	**C**	**D**	**E**

15 A sequence of numbers is written using the rule 'Starting with 24, halve the number and add 8'. What is the fourth number in the sequence?

12	20	18	19	17
A	**B**	**C**	**D**	**E**

16 Here is a net of a cube:

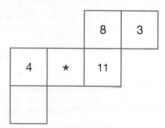

The net is folded to form a cube. Numbers on opposite faces have the same difference. Which of these could be the number represented by ⋆?

10	18	12	15	6
A	**B**	**C**	**D**	**E**

17 Which digit has been replaced with ▲ in this number sentence?

$$658 + 2▲5 = 903$$

5	1	3	4	2
A	B	C	D	E

18 Abbi planted a 60-cm tall shrub in her garden in September 2016. Each year the shrub has grown 30 cm taller. What was the height of the plant in September 2021?

A 2 m 1 cm

B 2 m 4 cm

C 2 m 10 cm

D 2 m 40 cm

E 4 m 50 cm

19 Isabella draws a square on a grid with side length 4 cm. She cuts out a rectangle measuring 2 cm by 1 cm from the square. Which of these could be the perimeter of the new shape?

A 14 cm

B 12 cm

C 10 cm

D 19 cm

E 20 cm

20 Rhys makes an average of 250 phone calls each month. Which of these is closest to the number of phone calls made each year?

A 2400   B 2600   C 2800

D 3000   E 3200

21 Donald is doing this puzzle.

Write the same whole number in each circle to make the number sentences true.

4 × ● is smaller than 25.

● + ● is bigger than 6.

Donald noticed that there is more than one correct answer to the puzzle.

How many different correct answers are there?

2	3	4	5	6
A	B	C	D	E

22 The diagram shows two pan balances. JayJay has placed cubes, spheres and cylinders on the balances.

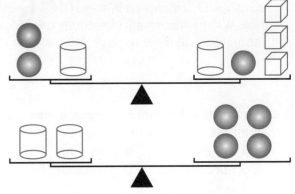

What is the mass of one cylinder?

A 1 sphere

B 3 spheres

C 2 cubes

D 3 cubes

E 6 cubes

23 Tedros is shading squares on the grid.

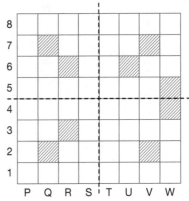

He wants the vertical and horizontal lines to be lines of symmetry where each square on the left reflects to a square on the right and each square on the top reflects to a square on the bottom. Which squares does Tedros need to shade?

A Q4, Q5, U3

B P4, Q5, U3

C Q4, Q5, U4

D P4, P5, U3

E Q4, Q5, U2

24 A supermarket sells rice in two different-sized bags. A small bag contains 500 g and costs $2. A larger bag contains 1.5 kg and costs $5. Dev wants to buy exactly 4 kg of rice. What is the smallest amount of money he will need to pay?

$15	$16	$18	$14	$20
A	B	C	D	E

25 What is the difference between a quarter of an hour and a fifth of an hour?

A 1 minute   **B** 2 minutes
C 3 minutes   **D** 4 minutes
E 5 minutes

26 The column graph shows the number of goals scored by Lauren's team in the first five games of a soccer season.

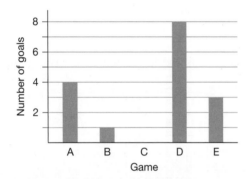

Lauren reads the graph and makes three claims:

1 The team scored three times more goals in game A as in game B.
2 The team scored fewer than five goals in four games.
3 The team scored a total of 15 goals in the five games.

Using the information on the graph, which of Lauren's claims is/are correct?

A claim 1 only
B claim 2 only
C claims 1 and 2 only
D claims 2 and 3 only
E claims 1, 2 and 3

27 Pedro added the number of lines of symmetry on a rectangle to the number of lines of symmetry on a triangle with only two equal sides. What is the total number?

6	7	5	4	3
A	B	C	D	E

28

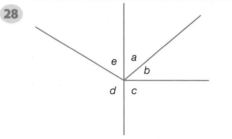

Which of these angles would measure about 120°?

a	*b*	*c*	*d*	*e*
A	B	C	D	E

29 Magda has a parallelogram.

She makes one straight-line cut to divide the parallelogram into two shapes. Which of these can she make with the one cut?

1 a triangle and a rectangle
2 two triangles
3 two quadrilaterals
A 1 only
B 2 only
C 3 only
D 1 and 2 only
E 2 and 3 only

30 Tessa is in the school playground. She is looking at Sebastian, who is north-east of her. A 6-m flagpole is 12 m south of Sebastian and east of Tessa. How far is Tessa from the flagpole?

6 m	18 m	8 m	10 m	12 m
A	B	C	D	E

31 A group of people were surveyed regarding their favourite citrus. The results of the survey are shown in the picture graph below.

orange	
mandarin	
lemon	
grapefruit	
tangelo	
	Key: = 4 people

Deepali reads the graph and makes three claims:

1 Nine students liked grapefruits or tangelos.
2 Twice as many liked mandarins as the number who liked lemons.
3 Thirty-six (36) people were surveyed.

Using the information on the graph, which of Deepali's claims is/are correct?

A claim 1 only
B claim 2 only
C claims 1 and 2 only
D claims 2 and 3 only
E claims 1, 2 and 3

32 The arrow on the spinner is spun twice. The results are added together and a score is calculated.

Which of these scores is **not** possible?

6	9	10	11	12
A	**B**	**C**	**D**	**E**

33 Which of the following solids has exactly five faces and nine edges?

A pentagonal prism
B triangular pyramid
C rectangular prism
D square pyramid
E triangular prism

34 Harvey looked at the reflection of the time on a clock in a mirror. Later he looked at the time again. Here are the two images. What is the time difference between the two times?

A 2 hours 20 minutes
B 2 hours 40 minutes
C 3 hours 20 minutes
D 3 hours 20 minutes
E 4 hours 20 minutes

35 A bag contains 10 balls. Four of the balls are red, three are blue and the remainder are green. Alf chooses a ball at random from the bag.

Which of these statements is/are correct?

1 A green ball is more likely to be chosen than a red ball.
2 A blue or green ball is twice as likely as a red ball to be chosen.
3 If a red ball is removed from the bag, a red, blue or green ball is equally likely to be chosen.

A statement 1 only
B statement 2 only
C statement 3 only
D statements 2 and 3 only
E statements 1, 2 and 3

1 The number in each of the squares is the result of adding the numbers in the nearest circles.

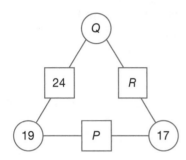

What is the sum of P, Q and R?

63	55	48	60	66
A	B	C	D	E

2 A rectangle has a length of 12 cm. The width is one-third the length. What is the perimeter of the rectangle?

A 32 cm
B 28 cm
C 15 cm
D 30 cm
E 16 cm

3 Here is a number line.

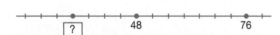

What is the missing number in the box?

28	30	32	34	36
A	B	C	D	E

4 Each row of the table has numbers that form a pattern.

2	4	6	A	10	12
3	7	11	B	19	23

What is $A + B$?

23	22	8	15	35
A	B	C	D	E

5 Olivia is using beads to make a necklace. For every two red beads, she is using three pink beads and a white bead. If she uses a total of 12 pink beads, how many red beads will she use?

6	8	9	12	18
A	B	C	D	E

6 Aaron used a calculator to find the answer to 146 + 287 + 329 + 45. He mistakenly typed 146 + 287 + 329 − 45. The answer on his calculator was 717. Which of these should have been the answer?

A 797
B 807
C 752
D 762
E 790

7 The shape is made from a square and a circle. How many lines of symmetry has this shape?

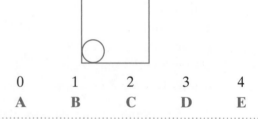

0	1	2	3	4
A	B	C	D	E

8 Two burgers and two bottles of soft drink cost $20. The cost of a burger and two bottles of soft drink is $13. What is the cost of three bottles of soft drink?

A $3
B $6
C $9
D $12
E $15

9 What is the difference in the values of the 6s in the number 2686?

A 600   B 606   C 596
D 594   E 706

10 Which of these is a square number with the smallest number of factors?

2	16	36	49	64
A	B	C	D	E

11 Altogether, Luke and Jacob have 24 golf balls. Jacob has half as many balls as Luke. How many more balls has Luke than Jacob?

4	6	8	12	16
A	B	C	D	E

12 Scott is given a $120 gift card for his birthday. He spends $40 on a phone cover and $30 on a vinyl record. Half of the remaining money is spent on a movie ticket. How much money remains on the gift card?

A $25

B $15

C $20

D $50

E $40

13 In this diagram, 6 + 5 = 11.

Here is a new diagram that works in the same way:

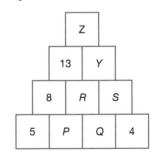

What is the number replacing *Z*?

21	22	23	24	25
A	B	C	D	E

14 The sum of two numbers is 48. If the smaller number is one-third of the larger number, what is the difference between the two numbers?

8	16	18	20	24
A	B	C	D	E

15 A total of 100 tickets for a school concert was sold. The ticket categories are listed below in the table. Only the number of tickets sold to seniors is recorded.

Category	Number
Adult	
Child	
Senior	10

The number of child tickets sold is three times the number of senior tickets. How many adult tickets were sold?

90	50	40	30	60
A	B	C	D	E

16 Here are the first four terms of a number sequence:

1, 3, 9, 27 …

What is the difference between the second and fifth terms in this sequence?

81	78	30	54	60
A	B	C	D	E

17 Pahadi has 20 mandarins. She gives five mandarins to her neighbour. She also gives each of her four friends three mandarins. Which number sentence can be used to find the number of mandarins she has left?

A $5 \times 4 + 3 - 20$

B $3 \times 4 + 5 - 20$

C $20 - 5 - 4 - 3$

D $20 - 5 - 4 \times 3$

E $5 + 4 \times 3 - 20$

18 Ms Stewart arranges eight students in each of 12 equal rows and then another seven students in a 13th row. Which of these number sentences is used to work out the total number of students?

A $8 \times 12 + 13 \times 7$

B $8 \times 13 - 7$

C $12 \times 13 - 8 + 7$

D $12 \times 8 + 13$

E $12 \times 8 + 7$

19 An isosceles triangle has two equal sides. Albert draws an isosceles triangle with a perimeter of 18 cm. If one of the sides is 8 cm long, which of these could be the length of another side?

A 3 cm   B 6 cm   C 4 cm

D 5 cm   E 10 cm

20 Jack has made a ruler using a length of cardboard. There are markings on his ruler showing 0 cm, 3 cm, 5 cm, 8 cm and 9 cm.

```
|       |       |       |   |   |
0       3       5       8   9
cm
```

Jack uses his ruler to measure some distances. Which of these lengths can he **not** accurately measure without moving his ruler?

1 cm   2 cm   4 cm   7 cm   9 cm

 A   B   C   D   E

21 The sign shows the business hours of Harvey's Pharmacy.

Harvey's Pharmacy
Opening hours
Monday – Friday 9 am – 6 pm
Saturday   10 am – 2 pm
Sunday   10 am – 1 pm

How many hours is the pharmacy open each week?

A 16 hours   B 51 hours   C 52 hours

D 53 hours   E 63 hours

22 Three friends weighed their dogs. The total mass of the three dogs is 68 kg. Willow's Jack Russell has a mass of 7 kg. Sam's German Shepherd is five times as heavy as the Jack Russell. What is the mass of Lincoln's Border Collie?

A 35 kg

B 24 kg

C 33 kg

D 61 kg

E 26 kg

23 Oscar has a dentist appointment at twenty past ten. He arrives 12 minutes early. His dentist is 7 minutes late. The appointment lasts 29 minutes. He left 3 minutes later. What time did Oscar leave?

A 11:11

B 11:09

C 10:51

D 10:59

E 11:01

24 The grid shows the journey taken by Mark. He started at *A* then walked north to *B*, east to *C*, south to *D*, west to *E* and south to *F*.

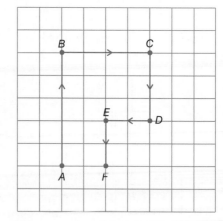

Altogether he walked 320 m. How far is he from where he started?

2 m   20 m   4 m   40 m   4 km

 A   B   C   D   E

25 Here is a shape:

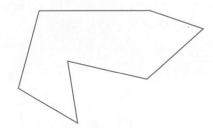

How many angles measure less than a right angle?

1	3	4	5	6
A	B	C	D	E

26 Mo is shading squares on the grid.

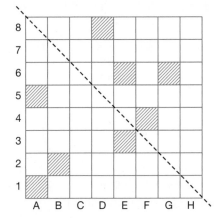

He wants the dotted line to be a line of symmetry where each square on one side of the line reflects to a square on the other side of the line. How many squares does Mo need to shade?

1	2	3	4	6
A	B	C	D	E

27 The mass of two crates is compared. Crate A has four times the mass of Crate B. If the total mass is 60 kg, what is the mass of the heavier crate?

A 12 kg

B 15 kg

C 45 kg

D 48 kg

E 50 kg

28 Macy's heart beats an average of 68 times a minute. Which of these is closest to the number of times Macy's heart beats between half past ten and 11 o'clock?

A 700

B 1000

C 1200

D 1500

E 2000

29 Ben has three acute angles. Which of these statements is/are correct?

1 The sum could be an acute angle.

2 The sum could be an obtuse angle.

3 The sum could be a reflex angle.

A statement 2 only

B statement 3 only

C statements 1 and 2 only

D statements 2 and 3 only

E statements 1, 2 and 3

30 Aleesha has a regular hexagon.

She makes one straight-line cut to divide the hexagon into two shapes. Which of these can she make with the one cut?

1 a triangle and a pentagon

2 two quadrilaterals

3 two pentagons

A 1, 2 and 3

B 1 and 2 only

C 1 and 3 only

D 2 and 3 only

E 1 only

31 Megan is facing west.
She does a quarter turn to the right.
Which direction is she now facing?

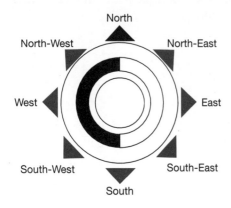

A north-west
B north
C south-west
D south
E east

32 Here is a sequence of numbers.

140, 136, 132, 128 ….

What is the largest two-digit number in the sequence?

104	99	98	96	95
A	B	C	D	E

33 Alice picked up a cube and counted all the right angles on the cube. How many angles did Alice count?

18	12	24	6	8
A	B	C	D	E

34 A group of students were asked for the number of their siblings. The results are recorded on the graph below.

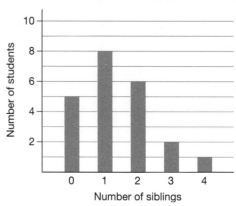

How many students had at least two siblings?

3	4	6	8	9
A	B	C	D	E

35 Here are four shapes.

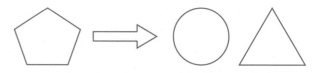

Elise organises the shapes into groups of two. How many different groups are possible?

3	6	8	9	12
A	B	C	D	E

SAMPLE TEST 12

40 MIN

1 Here are three squares, *P*, *Q* and *R*.

Square *P*   Square *Q*   Square *R*

Which of the squares has/have $\frac{3}{4}$ shaded?
A square *P* only
B square *Q* only
C square *R* only
D squares *P* and *Q* only
E squares *P*, *Q* and *R*

2 *A*, *B* and *C* represent digits in the sum below.

```
   C 2 4
   2 7 6
 + 3 B 2
 ───────
   7 6 A
```

What is the product of *A*, *B* and *C*?

12	16	18	36	56
A	B	C	D	E

3 The two rectangles below are joined to make one large rectangle.

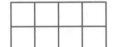   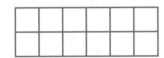

What is the perimeter of the new rectangle?
A 20 units
B 22 units
C 24 units
D 28 units
E 30 units

4 How many whole numbers greater than 30 but less than 100 can be written using only even digits?

20	12	15	16	25
A	B	C	D	E

5 Alphi makes a pattern using triangles and squares. If the pattern continues, how many triangles are in the shape with eight squares?

12	14	16	18	20
A	B	C	D	E

6 There were 120 marbles in a bag. Fifty of the marbles were green and the rest were red or blue. There were twice as many green marbles as blue. How many more green than red marbles were in the bag?

5	10	15	20	25
A	B	C	D	E

7 The sum of three numbers is 100. One of the numbers is 28. Another number is half of one of the numbers. Which of these could **not** be two of the numbers?
A 14 and 58
B 16 and 56
C 16 and 28
D 24 and 48
E 22 and 50

8 Thomas bought some pens which cost $5 each. He paid for the pens with a $50 note and received $15 in change. How many pens did Thomas buy?

3	5	10	8	7
A	B	C	D	E

9 In Australia, Mother's Day is on the second Sunday in May. Father's Day is on the first Sunday in September. How many days are there from Mother's Day to Father's Day?

118	119	120	121	122
A	B	C	D	E

10 Micah is to shade four more squares on the grid.
He wants the dotted line to be a line of symmetry.

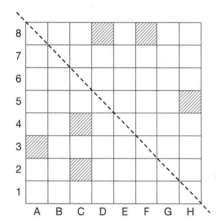

What are the grid references of the squares he needs to shade?

A F2, H3, G4 and D2
B E6, G6, A5 and D1
C H3, F2, D1 and C7
D E6, G6, A4 and D2
E F2, H3, A5 and D1

11 Here is a 6 by 4 grid. Three friends shaded parts of the grid.

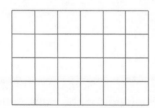

- Layla shaded $\frac{2}{3}$ of the grid squares.

- Grace shaded $\frac{1}{4}$ of the remaining unshaded squares.

- Finally, Willow shaded $\frac{5}{6}$ of the remaining unshaded squares.

How many squares on the grid remain unshaded?

0	1	2	3	6
A	B	C	D	E

12 The number in each of the squares is the result of adding the numbers in the nearest circles.

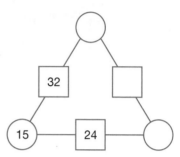

What is the sum of the three missing numbers?

46	50	57	52	61
A	B	C	D	E

13 The mass of a box of cereal and two cans of tomatoes is 1.7 kg. The mass of each can is 400 g. What is the mass of the box of cereal?

A 760 g
B 800 g
C 840 g
D 900 g
E 960 g

14 At 9:02, a tram leaves Town Hall. Every 7 minutes a tram departs the stop. How many trams have departed between 9:05 and 9:45?

4	5	6	7	8
A	B	C	D	E

15 Here are two sequences of numbers.
Sequence A: 3, 8, 13, 18, 23 …
Sequence B: 4, 10, 16, 22 …
Which of these numbers is in both sequences?

38	43	46	48	58
A	B	C	D	E

16 At 9 o'clock the hands of an analog clock form a right angle.

How many times in a 24-hour period do the hands of the clock form a right angle at a time when both hands are each pointing to numbers?

2	4	6	12	24
A	B	C	D	E

17 Rupert has a quadrilateral with two parallel sides and two other equal sides.

He makes one straight-line cut to divide the quadrilateral into two shapes. Which of these pairs can he make with the one cut?

1 a triangle and a quadrilateral
2 a trapezium and a parallelogram
3 a parallelogram and a triangle

A 1 and 2 only
B 1 and 3 only
C 2 and 3 only
D 1, 2 and 3
E 1 only

18 Here is a number line.

What is the value of $A + B - C$?

24	18	3	15	18
A	B	C	D	E

19 What same number should be used to replace the square to give a true number sentence?

$$14 \times \square - \square \times 4 = 80$$

6	16	10	12	8
A	B	C	D	E

20 Emma has made a ruler using a length of cardboard. There are markings on her ruler showing 0 cm, 2 cm, 4 cm, 5 cm, 7 cm and 10 cm.

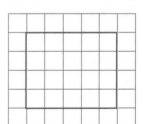

Emma uses her ruler to measure some distances. Which of these lengths can she **not** accurately measure without moving her ruler?

A 1 cm
B 3 cm
C 6 cm
D 8 cm
E 9 cm

21 Lily drew a rectangle on the grid below. The perimeter of the rectangle is 36 cm.

What is the area of the rectangle?
A 160 cm²
B 40 cm²
C 60 cm²
D 20 cm²
E 80 cm²

22 Aaron's family bought a very large pizza to share for dinner. Aaron ate $\frac{1}{4}$ of the pizza. The other members of the family ate $\frac{1}{8}$ of the pizza each. There was still $\frac{1}{4}$ of the pizza remaining. How many family members had dinner with Aaron?

1	2	3	4	5
A	B	C	D	E

23 Bethany has started to write the numbers 1 to 9 in the circles in this puzzle. Lines are drawn to join the three circles around the outside of the puzzle. The numbers in each of these three circles add to the same sum.

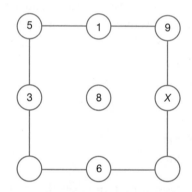

What number will replace the letter X?

2	4	7	3	1
A	B	C	D	E

24 Here are the first four terms of a number sequence:

$$6, 11, 16, 21 \dots$$

What is the difference between the sixth term and the 10th term in this sequence?

20	24	25	30	31
A	B	C	D	E

25 My sister is twice my age and my brother is three years younger than me. The product of our three ages is 100. How old is my brother?

1	2	4	5	10
A	B	C	D	E

26 The jug is nearly completely filled with water. One-third of the water is poured out. 200 mL is then added to the jug. Three-quarters of the water is then poured out.

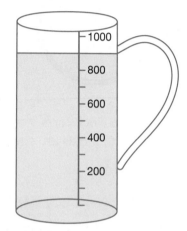

How much water remains in the jug?
A 300 mL
B 600 mL
C 200 mL
D 500 mL
E 400 mL

27 Grace has a pan balance and five blocks. The blocks have different masses: 15 kg, 10 kg, 8 kg, 5 kg and 2 kg. Grace used some of the blocks to measure the exact mass of a cylinder.

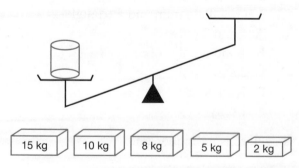

Which of these **cannot** be the mass of the cylinder?

17 kg	28 kg	22 kg	23 kg	24 kg
A	B	C	D	E

28 Dominic starts with a piece of paper in the shape of a parallelogram, as shown.

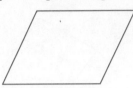

He makes **one fold** in the paper, without moving it in any other way.
Which of the following shapes could **not** be the result?

A

B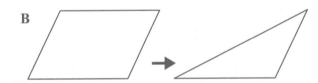

C

D

E

29 The picture graph shows the weekly amounts raised by five classes in a Winter Appeal.

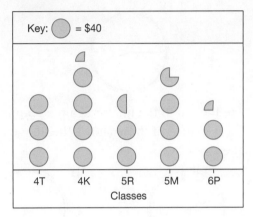

Min reads the graph and makes three claims:

1 Class 4K raised $170.
2 Class 4T raised $10 more than Class 5R.
3 Classes 5R and 5M raised a total of $250.

Using the information on the graph, which of Min's claims is/are correct?

A claims 1, 2 and 3
B claims 1 and 3 only
C claims 1 and 2 only
D claim 1 only
E claim 2 only

30 This shape is made from eight small, identical cubes.

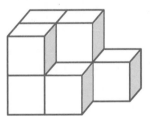

Connie picks up the shape and views it from all directions.
How many cube faces cannot be seen?

10	12	18	20	28
A	B	C	D	E

31 Ross looked at his kitchen clock in a mirror. This is the image that Ross could see.

He looked at the mirror again 90 minutes later. Which of these shows the image of the clock?

A   B

C

D   E

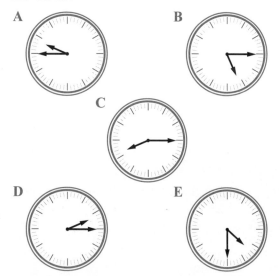

32 A triangle with three equal sides is drawn on the grid below.

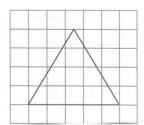

If the perimeter of the triangle is 30 cm, what is the scale used on the grid?

A 1 unit represents 1 cm
B 1 unit represents 2 cm
C 1 unit represents 5 cm
D 1 unit represents 6 cm
E 1 unit represents 10 cm

33 The diagram below shows a triangular prism.

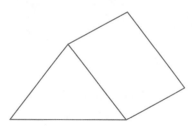

Noah picked up the prism and counted all the right angles on the solid. How many angles did Noah count?

16	4	8	20	12
A	B	C	D	E

34 Four students are to be arranged in a line to get on a bus. How many different arrangements of students are possible?

10	18	20	24	36
A	B	C	D	E

35 Students completed a quiz consisting of 20 questions. The graph shows the number of girls and boys who answered at least 15 questions correctly.

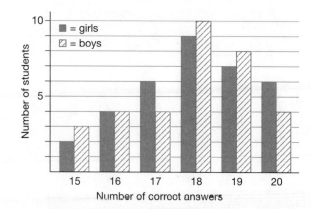

How many students answered at most three questions incorrectly?

23	78	44	55	54
A	B	C	D	E

SAMPLE Test 1 Page 1

> 1 B 2 B 3 C 4 A 5 D 6 A 7 C 8 A 9 B
> 10 C 11 E 12 C 13 D 14 E 15 E 16 B
> 17 B 18 A 19 E 20 E 21 E 22 C 23 D
> 24 D 25 B 26 C 27 D 28 B 29 D 30 A
> 31 D 32 E 33 B 34 D 35 E

1 $30 \div 6 = 5$ and $X = 4 \times 5 = 20$. Here is the completed puzzle.

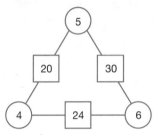

2 As 37 + 37 is 74, the pens cost $7.40. Ethan's change is $10 – $7.40 = $2.60.

3 The rule is the top number is subtracting 2 from the bottom number and then dividing this answer by 3. As 23 – 2 = 21 and 21 ÷ 3 = 7, the missing number is 7.

4 Call the friends A, B, C and D. A shakes hands with B, C and D. B then needs to shake hands only with C and D. C can only shake hands with D and D has by now shaken hands with every other person. 3 + 2 + 1 = 6.

5 Check the units column first: 8 – 3 = 5. For the tens column, 5 – □ = 9 cannot be done. So it needs to be 15 – □ = 9. This means the missing number must be 6.

6 Start with 36 and use the opposite operations. 36 ÷ 3 is 12, and then 12 – 7 = 5. The starting number is 5.

7 Adding 5, 2, 8, 1 and 6 gives 22. As 33 – 22 = 11, Grandpa should pay Tom $11.

8 Triple 11 is 11 × 3 = 33. As a dozen is 12, then 33 – 12 = 21.

9 690 is 10 away, 709 is 9 away, 800 is 100 away, 721 is 21 away and 770 is 70 away. The closest is 709.

10 11 oranges would cost $9.90 (11 × 90 = 990).

11 The factors are 4: 1, 2, 4; 8: 1, 2, 4, 8; 12: 1, 2, 3, 4, 6, 12; 14: 1, 2, 7, 14; 17: 1, 17. As 17 has only two factors (it is prime), it is the number with the smallest number of factors.

12 Ella gave half to her friend and kept half of the cake. She then gave a quarter of her half to her mother. This means she gave one-eighth of the cake to her mother.

13 As 16 – 2 = 14, Jacob has 14 balls. As 14 + 8 = 22, Lily has 22 balls. As 22 ÷ 2 = 11, Aiden has 11 balls.

14 There are 12 eggs in a dozen and six in half a dozen. 12 × 7 is 84 and adding six gives 90. There are 90 eggs.

15 As 2 × 3 = 6, then Y = 6. As 3 × 4 = 12, then Z = 12. As Y × Z = X and 6 × 12 = 72, the value of X is 72. Here is the completed diagram:

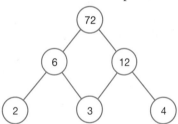

16 36 – 17 is 36 – 16 – 1 = 20 – 1 = 19. Bald Hill is 19 km closer than Dry Creek.

17 As 4 × 3 = 12, each wall has an area of 12 m². As 12 × 3 = 36, the total area to be painted is 36 m². As 36 ÷ 2 = 18, Logan will need 18 L.

18 A square pyramid has a square face and four triangles the same size as faces.

19 As 60 ÷ 3 = 20, every minute 20 mL falls into the bucket. As 60 × 20 = 1200, then 1200 mL is collected after one hour.

20 Change each mass to grams: 120 g, 1300 g, 87 g, 1004 g, 769 g. The order is 87 g, 120 g, 769 g, 1004 g, 1300 g. The middle mass is 769 g.

21 Seven students have two siblings. Claim 1 is not correct. As 7 + 0 + 2 = 9, there are nine students who have more than one sibling. Claim 2 is correct. As 4 + 10 + 7 + 0 + 2 = 23, and 25 – 23 = 2, there were two students absent. Claim 3 is correct. Claims 2 and 3 are correct.

22 If ▲ + ▲ is less than 16, the missing number is any whole number less than 8. If 12 + ▲ is bigger than 15, the missing number is any number bigger than 3. This means the correct answer could be 4, 5, 6 or 7. This means there are 4 correct answers.

23 6:55 to 7:55 =1 h, 7:55 to 8:00 = 5 min, 8:00 to 8:22 = 22 min. 5 + 22 = 27 min. The trip took 1 h 27 min.

24 Half a kilogram is 500 g. As 700 + 500 + 250 = 1450, the total mass is 1450 g.

25 By counting, or using 5 × 5, there are 25 small squares inside the large square. As 50 ÷ 25 = 2, each of these small squares has an area of 2 cm². As the shaded square covers 4 squares, and 4 × 2 = 8, the shaded square has an area of 8 cm².

26 There are five small triangles, as well as five larger triangles that each have a vertex at one of the points of the star shape. As 5 + 5 = 10, there are 10 triangles.

27 A has a diagonal line of symmetry, B has 6, C has 4 and E has a horizontal line of symmetry. Shape D does not have a line of symmetry.

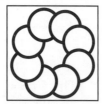

28 There are 60 minutes in 1 hour and 120 minutes in 2 hours. As 132 – 120 = 12, then 132 minutes is 2 hours 12 minutes. 7:55 plus 2 hours is 9:55. Another 12 minutes is adding 7 + 5 minutes so 5 minutes takes us to 10:00 pm and another 7 minutes gives the answer of 10:07. The movie finishes at 10:07 pm.

29 As 1 + 2 + 2 + 1 + 3 + 1 = 10, there are 10 coloured pencils. As there are three yellow pencils, the chance it is yellow is 3 chances in 10.

30 The area of the vertical cross-section will be a circle.

31 There are two 3-cm triangles. Their total edge length is 2 × 9 cm (18 cm). There are three 5-cm long sides: 3 × 5 cm = 15 cm. 18 cm + 15 cm = 33 cm.

32 The three squares are located at C1, G3 and E6. Here is the completed grid:

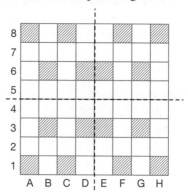

33 The stack is 3 blocks wide and 3 blocks long. It has to be 3 blocks high to make it into a cube (27 cubes). 27 – 9 = 18.

34 At 4 pm the temperature was 15°, which was not higher than the temperature at 9 am (17°). Claim 1 is not correct. At 7 am the temperature was 9°, which was half the temperature at 10 am (18°). Claim 2 is correct. At 8 am the temperature was 12°. By midday the temperature was 22°. As 22 – 12 = 10, the temperature increased by 10°. Claim 3 is correct. Claims 2 and 3 are correct.

35 From *D* to *A* is 2 units and from A to B is 4 units. As 2 + 4 = 6, Drew has walked 6 units. This means 6 units represents 300 m. As 30 ÷ 6 = 5, then 300 ÷ 6 = 50. Each unit on the grid equals 50 m. From *D* to *E* is 3 units, *E* to *F* is 4 units and *F* to *C* is 2 units. As 3 + 4 + 2 = 9, Drew walked 9 units. As 9 × 5 = 45, 9 × 50 = 450. Drew walked 450 m on Sunday.

SAMPLE Test 2   Page 7

1 E 2 D 3 B 4 B 5 B 6 E 7 D 8 B 9 C
10 C 11 D 12 C 13 D 14 A 15 A 16 D
17 C 18 E 19 B 20 D 21 B 22 B 23 E
24 D 25 A 26 E 27 D 28 D 29 E 30 B
31 A 32 B 33 C 34 C 35 D

1 16 257 has a 2 in the hundreds place. Subtracting 2 hundreds from 16 257 will give 16 057. Subtracting another 2 hundreds will give 15 857.

2 Four 50-cent coins is $2. $4.20 – $2.00 is $2.20. This means Brittany has 11 20-cent coins.

3 As 12 × 6 = 72, there are 72 eggs in 6 dozen. As 72 – 7 = 65, there are 65 remaining.

4 At the moment the abacus has 0 ten-thousands, 5 thousands, 0 hundreds, 2 tens and 6 units. Barry needs 1 more ten-thousands, 2 thousands, 1 hundred, 3 tens and 2 units. He will put the most beads onto the tens spike.

5 Ginger has one 50c coin, four 20c coins, two 10c coins and five 5c coins.
As 50 + 80 + 20 + 25 = 175, Ginger has $1.75.

6 The multiples are 12, 15 and 18. 12 + 18 is 30 and then plus 15 gives 45.

7 As 4 × 4 = 16, there are 16 small rectangles in the shape. Seven out of 16 rectangles are shaded. This is written as $\frac{7}{16}$.

8 The total for each line/column/diagonal is 15.
15 – 9 – 2 = 4

9 The pattern of numbers is formed by subtracting 1, then subtracting 2, then 3, then 4, and so on. As 50 – 5 = 45, the next number is 45.

10 Pictures are on pages 2, 5, 8, 11, 14, 17, 20, 23, 26, 29 and 32. Eleven pages have pictures on them.

11 A tricycle has three wheels and a skateboard has four wheels. So multiply 2 by 3 and 3 by 4. Then add these results. This means the number sentence is 2 × 3 + 3 × 4.

12 A has four axes of symmetry, B 1, C 0 D 1 and E 1. C has none.

13 There are: one large rectangle, four small rectangles and four double rectangles (two vertical and two horizontal). This is a total of nine rectangles.

14 21 – 1 = 20. 20 ÷ 4 = 5. The solution would be:
5 + 5 + 5 + 5 + 1 = 21.

15 The shape is a large rectangle with length of 8 cm and width of 4 cm. As 8 + 8 + 4 + 4 = 24, the perimeter is 24 cm.

16 $\frac{1}{2}$ is the same as $\frac{2}{4}$. Add up the pizza that was eaten: $\frac{3}{4} + \frac{1}{4} + \frac{2}{4} + \frac{3}{4}$. This is a total of $\frac{9}{4}$, or $2\frac{1}{4}$.
As $3 - 2\frac{1}{4} = \frac{3}{4}$, then $\frac{3}{4}$ of a pizza remains.

17 There are eight 4 cm sides (= 32 cm) and four short sides of 2 cm (= 8 cm).
32 cm + 8 cm = 40 cm.

18 This is a squaring pattern. $7^2 = 49$. $X = 49$

19 The shape would be an oval (or ellipse).

20 There is 1 cm above, below, on the left and on the right of the picture. The dimensions are (6 – 1 – 1) × (5 – 1 – 1) or 4 × 3.

21 There are 2 halves in a whole. As 8 × 2 = 16, there are 16 halves in 8. There are 3 thirds in a whole. As 6 × 3 = 18, there are 18 thirds in 6. As 18 – 16 = 2, the difference is 2.

22 The tank is about one-quarter full. Divide by 4 to get a quarter of 60 L. There is about 15 L in the tank.

23 As 20 – 5 = 15, the cakes cost a total of $15. You need to work out $15 divided by 6. As 12 ÷ 6 = 2, and $3 ÷ 6 is 50c, each cake cost $2.50.

24 As 40 + 30 + 40 = 110, the total was $110.

25 Half the marbles are red so the chance is 1 in 2.

26 Five out of the 12 boxes, or five-twelfths of the shape, are shaded.

27 January has 31 days. If 1 January is a Saturday, then 4 weeks (28 days) later will be Saturday 29 January. Three days later (1 February) will be a Tuesday.

28 As 28 ÷ 4 = 7, Elsie had seven $2 coins. As 28 – 7 = 21, Elsie had 21 $1 coins. As 7 × 2 = 14 and 14 + 21 = 35, Elsie had a total of $35.

29 If you remove an equal amount from each side, you can take one large block and three small blocks from each side of the balance. You can see that with what is left, 1 large block = 4 small blocks. The large block must have a mass of 4 × 250 g = 1000 g = 1 kg.

30 Use something like your finger to compare the distances. The distance from the doorway to the window is about three times the width of the bed. The distance is about 3 m.

31 From 1988 to 2000 is 12 years and then to 2017 is another 17 years. As 12 + 17 = 29, Ken would have been 29 on 5 June 2017. But Ken hadn't had his birthday in January 2017 so he was still 28.

32 Looking from Palm Coast, Big Smoke Mt is above and to the left. This means I would have to travel in a north-westerly direction.

33 The two rectangles have four right angles each. There are also four right angles at each of the two points of intersection of the rectangles. As 8 + 4 + 4 = 16, there is a total of 16 right angles.

34 There are three layers in the shape. The bottom layer has eight cubes, the middle layer has four cubes and the top layer has two cubes. As 8 + 4 + 2 = 14, there are 14 cubes in the shape.

35 As 5 + 3 + 6 + 2 + 3 = 19, the graph has 19 squares. As 19 × 2 = 38, there were 38 members surveyed.

SAMPLE Test 3

Page 13

1 B 2 D 3 E 4 D 5 B 6 E 7 E 8 B 9 E
10 E 11 C 12 B 13 C 14 C 15 D 16 A
17 D 18 E 19 D 20 D 21 A 22 C 23 B
24 C 25 D 26 A 27 C 28 C 29 E 30 A
31 E 32 A 33 C 34 C 35 D

1 First, in the units column, 7 + 8 + 6 = 21. Now for the tens column. 2 + 5 + 9 + $\square$ = 18. As 18 − 16 = 2, the missing number is 2.

2 The even numbers are 6 and 8. To find the product you need to multiply: 6 × 8 = 48.

3 $2.35 and $1.75 is $2 + $1 + 30c + 70c + 5c + 5c = $4.10. Subtracting this from $10 gives $5.90.

4 Numbers that are multiples of 3 and 4 are also multiples of 12. The next multiple of 12 bigger than 40 is 48.

5 There are 49 squares in the crossword. 15 are black. 15 is one-third of 45.

6 There are 20 squares. Dividing the shape into fifths means there will be four squares in each of the fifths. As 3 × 4 = 12, there will be 12 squares shaded.

7 The time on the clock is 4:35. You need to work out the number of hours and minutes in 435 minutes. As 7 × 6 = 42, then 7 × 60 = 420. Adding another 15 is 435. This means there are 7 h 15 min in 435 min. Adding 7 h to 4:35 is 11:35 and then another 15 min is 11:50.

8 In option B, four 20c coins is 80c. $2 + 80c + 5c = $2.85

9 As 5 × 3 + 8 = 23, then 7 × 4 + missing number = 42. This means the missing number is 42 − 28 = 14.

10 As 7 + 12 + 5 = 24, the sum of each row, column and diagonal is 24. Here is the final square. The missing number is 6.

11	4	9
6	8	10
7	12	5

11 Start by multiplying by 2, then 3, then 4, and so on. 5 × 24 = 120.

12 The change from $5 will be $2.60. The smallest number of coins would be a 10-cent coin, a 50-cent coin and a $2 coin. This would be three coins.

13 Start with the answer and work backwards. 19 − 9 = 10. This means $\square$ − 12 = 10. Now 10 + 12 = 22 so $\square$ = 22.

14 The two temperatures are 32 °C and 6 °C. As 32 − 6 = 26, the difference is 26 °C.

15 The first number is multiplied by 1 to give the second number. The second number is multiplied by 2 to give the third number. The third number is multiplied by 3, and so on. This means 1 × 1 = **1**, 1 × 2 = **2**, 2 × 3 = **6**, 6 × 4 = **24**, 24 × 5 = **120**. The next number is 120.

16 There are 12 squares in shape A, which is the most. B has 11, C has 10, D has 10 and E has four.

17 Three girls have birthdays in April. There are no girls' birthdays in March, June and September. In April and October, there are 3 girls' birthdays. There are 7 spring birthdays but 8 summer birthdays. There are 15 birthdays in the second half of the year compared to 12 birthdays in the first half of year.

18 Half ($\frac{1}{2}$) the numbers are even; that is, 1 in every two, or 1 chance in 2.

19 Half of 5 cm is 2.5 cm. The perimeter is adding two lengths and two widths. This means add double 5 and double 2.5. As 10 + 5 = 15, the perimeter is 15 cm.

20 There are 12 cherry tomatoes. To find the number of quarters, multiply by 4. 12 × 4 = 48.

21 Jill needs 8 asparagus spears for 4 people. That is 2 spears per person. For 6 people she will need: 2 × 6 spears = 12 spears.

22 The tin has 1 kg (1000 g). The recipe requires 450 g. 1000 − 450 = 550, so 550 g.

23 There are five weekdays in each of four weeks and two in the last week. 5 × 4 is 20 plus 2 is 22. Now subtract Monday 8 June, which leaves 21 days.

24 (5 + 5 + 5 = 15). X can only equal 1. The answer to this question is greater than 10 as it is a two-digit number: XW. Three single-digit numbers that are all the same, and give a total greater than 10, must range between 4 and 9. As the two-digit number ends with the same number as on the left side of the equation (W), the only possible value for W = 5.

25 The opposite sides of a kite are different lengths. A triangle only has three sides. A rectangle has four right angles. This means the shape is a parallelogram. Remember: A rectangle is a parallelogram but here Rowan's shape has no right angles.

26 Here is a diagram showing the direction walked:

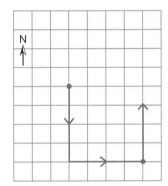

The hiker walked south, then east and finally north.

27 The angle is greater than a right angle (3 o'clock) but less than a straight angle (6 o'clock). It is an angle between 90° and 180°.

28 A hexagonal prism has eight faces and 18 edges. As 18 − 8 = 10, the difference is 10.

29 19 − 13 = 6, which means that Esther is six days older than Andy. Six days before Saturday is Sunday. Esther will have her birthday on a Sunday.

30 There are 1000 mL in 1 L. This means there are 2.5 L in 2500 mL.

31 The view is of a triangle on a square. A triangular prism has two triangular faces and a cube has six square faces.

32 A quarter turn clockwise three times will give the same shape as a quarter turn anticlockwise. This means the image will be like this:

33 If 4 cm represents 8 km on the map, the scale is 1 cm represents 2 km. As 6 ÷ 2 = 3, the goldmine and the dead tree are 3 cm apart.

34 Ethan is 24. As one-third of 24 is 24 ÷ 3 = 8, then two-thirds of 24 is 8 × 2 = 16. Liam is 16 years old. As 16 ÷ 4 = 4 and 4 × 5 = 20, Olivia is 20 years old.

35 Joy read 7 and Ben read 4. 7 − 4 = 3, so Joy read three more books than Ben. Claim 1 is correct. As Sky read 14, Rae 11, Zoe 5 and 14 is not more than 11 + 5 = 16, claim 2 is not correct. As 7 is half of 14, claim 3 is correct. Claims 1 and 3 are correct.

SAMPLE Test 4 Page 18

> 1 A 2 B 3 D 4 B 5 C 6 C 7 E 8 D 9 E
> 10 D 11 B 12 A 13 A 14 E 15 D 16 E
> 17 E 18 E 19 D 20 C 21 D 22 A 23 D
> 24 D 25 C 26 D 27 A 28 C 29 D 30 D
> 31 A 32 A 33 C 34 A 35 B

1 As 10 + 7 + 4 = 21, the sum of each row, column and diagonal is 21. Here is the final square. The missing number is 11.

10	3	8
5	7	9
6	11	4

2 Look at the numbers in the series. 3 **+ 2** = 5, then 5 **+ 3** = 8. Then repeat: 8 **+ 2** = 10, then 10 **+ 3** = 13, and so on. The rule is add 2, then add 3 and repeat.

3 Andre has 17 × 10 = 170. Brett has 17. 170 + 17 = 187. They have 187 cards altogether.

4 Start with 22 and use the opposite operations. 22 + 3 is 25, and 25 ÷ 5 is 5. The starting number is 5.

5 The sum of the length and width is 12 cm. This means the dimensions are 8 cm and 4 cm. As 8 × 4 = 32, the area is 32 cm².

6 Two dozen = 24. As 24 ÷ 6 = 4, Halle buys four bags of lemons. $2.10 × 4 = $8.40. As $10 – $8.40 = $1.60, Halle is given change of $1.60.

7 14 is not a multiple of 4. All the other numbers are multiples of 4.

8 There are 10 out of 12 pieces remaining. This can be written as $\frac{10}{12}$, which equals $\frac{5}{6}$.

9 Look at the middle row of numbers. As 4 and 7 are two large numbers, the other number in the row will have to be small. Try 1. As 1 + 4 + 7 = 12, the row/column total in the puzzle will be 12. As 12 – 6 – 1 = 5, X is replaced with 5. Here is the solved puzzle:

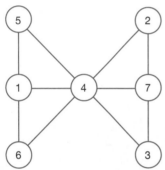

10 There will be 2 ten-thousands, 1 thousand, 1 hundred, 4 tens and 1 unit. This is the number 21 141, which is twenty-one thousand, one hundred and forty-one.

11 First, 75 ÷ 5 is 15. As 15 × 2 = 30, Mrs Scott can buy 30 bowls.

12 As $8 × 6 = $48 and 50c × 6 = $3, the total cost is $51. As 60 – 51 = 9, the change is $9.

13 The rule is subtracting 9. As 259 – 9 = 250, the missing number is 250.

14 As 24 ÷ 3 = 8, there are eight children on the bus. As 24 – 8 = 16, there are 16 adults.

15 As 3 + 2 + 1 = 6, then 2 out of 6 beads are red. This means $\frac{1}{3}$ of the beads are red. As 54 ÷ 3 = 18, there are 18 red beads.

16 First, 15 + 4 = 19. The number sentence is now $\square$ – 9 = 19. This means the missing

number is 9 more than 19. As 19 + 9 = 28, the missing number is 28.

17 As 10 + 8 = 18 and 12 + 4 = 16, the missing dimensions are 18 cm and 16 cm. The perimeter is twice the sum of 18 and 16. As 34 × 2 = 68, the perimeter is 68 cm.

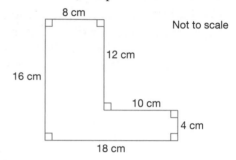

18 Edward's father has a mass that is 38 + 38 + half of 38. As 76 + 19 = 95, Edward's father has a mass of 95 kg.

19 Many clocks and watches do not have numerals. You can see the winding mechanism is on the right. This means the minute hand is pointing down to 6 and the hour hand is pointing between 8 and 9. The time is half past 8.

20 As 14 – 6 = 8, after the first hour Troy still has 8 km to run. If he runs this distance at 4 km per hour, it will take him 2 hours. As 1 + 2 = 3, Troy will take 3 hours.

21 1.25 mL is equal to 1250 mL. As twice 250 is 500, then four lots of 250 is 1000. Another 250 make 1250. This means Karen can fill five glasses.

22 The mass of 6 balls is the same as 1 ball + 10 kg. This means the mass of 5 balls = 10 kg and so each ball has a mass of 2 kg. As 2 × 2 = 4, the total mass is 4 kg.

23 There are 21 days in 3 weeks and 31 days in August. If 21 – 14 = 7, his anniversary was 7 days before the end of August. 31 – 7 = 24, so Joel's anniversary was on 24 August.

24 Imagine rotating the small piece so that the edges match.

25 Notice the direction of north on the map. The airstrip is to the right of Oru Beach on the map and so is east of Oru Beach.

26 On the map it is about 4 cm from the Coconut Oil Factory to Tarukua Beach. According to the scale, the distance would be about 8 km. (2 × 4 km = 8 km.)

27 Half a kilometre = 500 m

28 From 1:05 pm, subtract 5 minutes to get 1:00 pm and then subtract another 10 minutes to give 12:50 pm.

29 If 14 – ⬤ is more than 5, the missing number is any whole number less than 9. If ⬤ + ⬤ is bigger than 6, the missing number is any number bigger than 3. This means the correct answer could be 4, 5, 6, 7 or 8. This means there are 5 correct answers.

30 The graph shows a quarter of the people were born in Queensland. As 8 × 4 = 32, there were 32 people surveyed.

31 Here is the image alongside the original:

mirror line

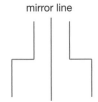

32 Shape P has two right angles, Q has none, R has four and S has one. Suppose shapes P and R were chosen. This leaves shapes Q and S with a total of one right angle.

33 Halfway between 2000 and 2500 is 2250. Claim 1 is correct. As 3000 – 2500 = 500, Sarah spent $500 more in week 4 than in week 2. Claim 2 is correct.
As 1500 + 2500 + 2250 = 6250, she spent a total of $6250 in weeks 1, 2 and 3. Claim 3 is not correct. Claims 1 and 2 are correct.

34 Three of the six numbers are odd. This is 3 chances in 6, which can be rewritten as 1 chance in 2.

35

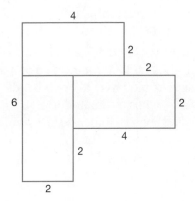

As 6 + 4 + 2 + 2 + 2 + 4 + 2 + 2 = 24, the perimeter is 24 cm.

SAMPLE Test 5 Page 24

1 C	**2** A	**3** E	**4** C	**5** B	**6** B	**7** E	**8** D	**9** D
10 A	**11** B	**12** B	**13** E	**14** A	**15** C	**16** E		
17 D	**18** E	**19** B	**20** D	**21** D	**22** B	**23** A		
24 E	**25** D	**26** D	**27** E	**28** C	**29** A	**30** D		
31 E	**32** D	**33** D	**34** D	**35** E				

1 1 uses one 1. The 10 numbers from 10 to 19 use one 1 except for 11, which uses two 1s. This means 12 1s are used.

2 To work out the number of pages in a chapter, subtract the opening page number of the following chapter from the opening page number of the chapter you want to know the page count of. So the number of pages in Temples of Chiang Mai is 19 – 14 = 5. Eating Out in Town has 30 – 27 = 3, District Tours has 27 – 23 = 4, The People has 8 – 5 = 3 and Historic Monuments has only one page.

3 As 60 + 40 + 60 + 40 = 200, the perimeter of the park is 200 m. As 200 ÷ 20 = 10, there will be 10 trees planted. Alternatively, four trees are planted along each long side and one in the middle of the short sides. This means 10 trees will be planted.

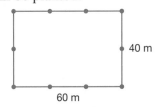

40 m

60 m

4 As $5 \times 8 = 40$, the value of X is 40.
As $40 \div 10 = 4$, the value of Y is 4.
As $40 - 4 = 36$, the difference is 36.

5 The amount shown is $3.35. The least number of coins required to make $10.00 will be: $1 \times 5c$, $1 \times 10c$, $1 \times 50c$, $3 \times \$2$. Total coins = 6

6 A multiple of 4 and 5 is 20. This means that all multiples of 20 are multiples of 4 and 5. So Kelsey could have 20 or 40 beads. Now, 40 divided by 6 has a remainder of 4, which means Kelsey has 40 beads. (20 divided by 6 only has a remainder of 2.)

7 As $12 + 18 = 30$ and $30 \div 2 = 15$, then half the sum is 15.

8 Elle's sister has $12. Elle has half as much again: ($12 + $6 = $18). $18 + $12 = $30

9 Chloe is given half (which is two-quarters) and Hudson one-quarter of the balls. This means Leo is given the remaining one-quarter of the balls. As $80 \div 4 = 20$, Leo receives 20 balls. Alternatively, as $80 \div 2 = 40$, Chloe is given 40 balls. As $80 \div 4 = 20$, Hudson is given 20 balls. As $40 + 20$ is 60 and $80 - 60$ is 20, Leo receives 20 balls.

10 A reflection in a mirror is a reflection about a vertical line.

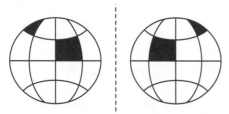

11 $4 plus 2×10 is $4 + $20 = $24.

12 There are 4 quarters in 1. As $6 \times 4 = 24$, there are 24 quarters.

13 As $18 - 7 = 11$ and $11 - 8 = 3$, $X = 11 + 3 = 14$. Here is the completed puzzle:

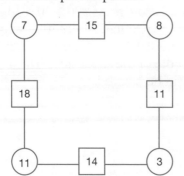

14 Glen 'high fived' Robert and then Jim. Robert 'high fived' Jim. This means there were three 'high fives'.

15 The numbers in the pattern are decreasing by 10, then 9, then 8, then 7, and so on. $105 - \mathbf{10} = 95$, $95 - \mathbf{9} = 86$, $86 - \mathbf{8} = 78$, and so on. The missing number is 86.

16 $100 \div 8$ is the same as $25 \div 2$. This means 25 km uses 2 L of petrol. As $25 \times 10 = 250$, Harine can drive 250 km.

17 W has 1 line of symmetry, B has 1, H has 2 and T has 1. The letter P does not have a line of symmetry.

18 12 kg + ball is heavier than 15 kg + cube. If the mass of ball = 6 kg and mass of cube = 2 kg, the total masses are 18 kg and 17 kg. As 18 is greater than 17, the left side would be heavier. Here is another method: as $15 - 12 = 3$, the ball is more than 3 kg heavier than the cube. This means the mass of ball = 6 kg and mass of cube = 2 kg.

19 The bottom number is the square of the top number plus 1. This means $5^2 + 1$ is $25 + 1 = 26$.

20 Try each of the options. As 4×4 is 16 and $16 - 3 = 13$, the number sentence is $4 \times 4 - 3$. The missing signs are $\times$ and $-$.

21 The rectangle has side lengths 4 units and 3 units. As $4 + 3 + 4 + 3 = 14$, the perimeter is 14 units. As 14 units = 28 cm, then 1 unit = 2 cm. The square has side lengths 4 units, which is 8 cm. As $8 \times 4 = 32$, the perimeter is 32 cm.

22 As $680 - 240 = 440$ and $440 \div 2 = 220$, the mass of an orange is 220 g. As $240 + 220 = 460$, the total mass is 460 g.

23 20 days after any Friday is 2 weeks and 6 days later (or 1 day less than 3 weeks later). The day must be a Thursday. The date is not important to the question.

24 Consider a hexagonal prism. As a hexagon has 6 sides and $6 \times 3 = 18$, a hexagonal prism has 18 edges. As a decagon has 10 sides and $10 \times 3 = 30$, a decagonal prism has 30 edges.

25 From 10:40 am to 11:00 am is 20 minutes. To 7:00 pm is 8 more hours and then to 7:15 pm is another 15 minutes. This is a total of 8 hours 35 minutes.

26 Option A: The shape is rotated a quarter turn in a clockwise direction. Option B: The shape is rotated a quarter turn in an anticlockwise direction. Option C: The shape is rotated a half turn. Option E: This is the same as Tegan's original (it may have been rotated a complete revolution). The shape that could not be Tegan's is Option D.

27 The tallest student is Ben at 151 cm. The shortest student is Don at 139 cm. As 51 – 39 is 12, then 151 – 139 = 12. The difference is 12 cm.

28 $3 = 300 cents. Now, 300 ÷ 4 is the same as 150 ÷ 2 = 75. Each child receives 75 cents.

29 Half of 12 is 6 and half of 8 is 4. As 12 + 8 + 6 + 4 + 12 + 8 + 6 + 4 = 60, the perimeter is 60 cm.

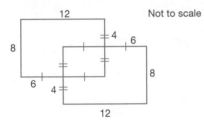

30 E has 4 right angles, F has 3, H has 4, L has 1, T has 2 and Z has 0. As 4 + 4 = 8, the highest possible number is 8 when E and H are chosen.

31 There are 4 units from P to Q. As 4 units represents 8 km and 8 ÷ 4 = 2, then 1 unit represents 2 km. Now count the units: P to Q is 4 units, Q to S is 4 units and S to R is 3 units. As 4 + 4 + 3 = 11 and 11 × 2 = 22, the total distance is 22 km.

32 There are 15 minutes in a quarter of an hour. 15 × 8 is 10 × 8 plus 5 × 8. As 80 + 40 = 120, they sell 120 programs each. As 120 × 2 = 240, they sell a total of 240 programs.

33 There are 8 lengths of 2 cm and 4 lengths of 8 cm. As 8 × 2 = 16, 8 × 4 = 32 and 32 + 16 = 48, the total length is 48 cm.

34 As three symbols represent 12 students, each symbol represents four students. This means 14 students nominated soccer and six students nominated netball. As 14 – 6 = 8, soccer was preferred over netball by eight more students.

35 There are 21 dots on a normal dice. (6 + 5 + 4 + 3 + 2 + 1 = 21). There are two dice (42 dots). 13 dots can be seen. 42 – 13 = 29.

SAMPLE Test 6   Page 29

1 C 2 D 3 D 4 E 5 E 6 E 7 B 8 C 9 C
10 D 11 D 12 D 13 B 14 B 15 E 16 A
17 B 18 E 19 E 20 E 21 C 22 C 23 E
24 D 25 E 26 E 27 E 28 E 29 E 30 C
31 E 32 D 33 A 34 D 35 E

1 76 is 24 from 100, 119 is 19 from 100, 245 is 45 from 200, 378 is 22 from 400 and 483 is 17 from 500. This means 245 changes the most.

2 The number is 160 divided by 8, which is 20.

3 As 20 ÷ 4 = 5, then 200 ÷ 4 = 50. As 220 = 200 + 20, then 220 ÷ 4 = 55. Each friend paid $55.

4 As 150 – 110 = 40 and 40 ÷ 3 is 13 with remainder 1, there are 13 numbers.

5 As 12 × 4 = 48, the number is 48. As 48 × 2 = 96, twice the number is 96.

6 There will be four squares that remain unshaded.

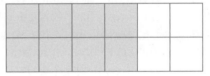

7 27 – 3 is 24 and half of 24 is 12. There are 12 girls (and 15 boys).

8 There were four lots of three wattles sold and so there were four lots of two roses sold: 4 × 2 = 8.

9 From 7:25 there are 35 minutes to 8:00. As 45 – 35 = 10, Lucas will have until 8:10.

10 Z has no line of symmetry. M, D and E have one line of symmetry. I has two lines of symmetry.

11 The number line is split into eighths. As $\frac{3}{4}$ is the same as $\frac{6}{8}$, the letter is D.

12 This shape was formed using two folds.

13 There are 12 full squares and two half squares shaded. Also, half of two squares is also shaded. As 12 + 1 + 1 = 14, and 14 × 2 = 28, the area is 28 cm².

14 As 1 + 6 = 7 and 1 + 5 = 6, the left corner number will be 1 less than the right corner number. Here is the solved puzzle. The total will be 9.

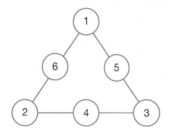

15 The pattern is repeating 'multiplying by 3, followed by dividing by 2'. As 9 × 3 = 27, the sixth number is 27. As 27 ÷ 2 = $13\frac{1}{2}$, the seventh number is $13\frac{1}{2}$.

16 This question could be solved in two different ways. Each pair of rows has five shaded squares. This means Denise will shade five squares. Another method is to find a number in the two rows that is divisible by 4. 16 is divisible by 4 so 160 is also divisible by 4. This means 152, 156, 160, 164 and 168 will be shaded.

17 As 80 + 80 + 50 + 50 = 160 + 100 = 260, the distance around one circuit is 260 m. As 260 × 4 = 1040, Symon ran a total distance of 1040 m.

18 Work in reverse with opposite operations. 18 − 10 + 7 − 8 = 7. Ingrid started with 7.

19 10 × 36 = 5 × 2 × 4 × 9. This can be written as 5 × 8 × 9. The missing number is 8.

20 There are four squares that are shaded. As 12 ÷ 4 = 3, each square has an area of 3 cm². There are six unshaded squares. As 6 × 3 = 18, the area is 18 cm².

21 6 L is 6000 mL and 6000 ÷ 300 is 60 ÷ 3 = 20. It will take 20 bottles to fill the container. If it takes half a minute to fill the bucket, it takes 1 minute to fill and empty two bottles. As 20 ÷ 2 = 10, it will take Mila 10 minutes.

22 If you take one cylinder off each side, you can see the mass of two cylinders is 8 kg. This means four cylinders have a total mass of 16 kg.

23 P + 6 = 9 which means P = 3. Also, 4 + Q = 11 which means Q = 7. The missing numbers are 6 + 4 = 10 and 10 + 11 = 21. This means 19 + 21 = R and so R = 40. The sum of P, Q and R is 3 + 7 + 40 = 50. Here is the solved diagram:

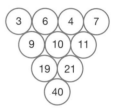

24 As 4 × 3 = 12 and 2 × 3 = 6, the dimensions of the rectangle are 12 cm by 6 cm. As 12 × 6 = 72, the area is 72 cm².

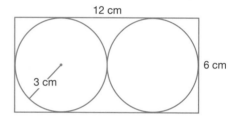

25 As 320 − 200 = 120, half of the strawberry jam has a mass of 120 g. As 120 × 2 = 240, all the jam has a mass of 240 g. As 320 − 240 = 80, the empty jar has a mass of 80 g.

26 7 × 5 = 35 and there are 31 days in May. Ella was born 4 days after 15 June. Ella's birthday is on 19 June.

27 There are 12 Eagles supporters and 48 Swans supporters (four times as many) so statement 1 is correct. There are 40 Dogs supporters and 24 Cats supporters, so there are fewer than twice as many students supporting the Dogs. Statement 2 is not correct. There are 28 Tigers, 48 Swans and 24 Cats supporters. As 28 + 48 + 24 = 100, statement 3 is correct. Statements 1 and 3 are correct.

28 In the first fold, J is behind the G. After the second fold, F and K are also behind the G.

29 B5 and E5 are 3 units apart. As 24 ÷ 3 = 8, each unit on the grid represents 8 m. D1 and D8 are 7 units apart. As 8 × 7 = 56, the distance between the two trees is 56 m.

30 There are two squares and each square has four right angles. Also there are four right angles outside the squares. As 2 × 4 is 8 and 8 + 4 = 12, there are 12 right angles.

31 There are 12 edges on a cube. As 12 × 4 = 48, the cube is made using 48 cm of wire.

32 Elijah moves two red balls from Bag 2 to Bag 1, one blue ball from Bag 1 to Bag 2 and three green balls from Bag 2 to Bag 1. As 2 + 1 + 3 = 6, Elijah moves 6 balls.

33 From the sketch below, the campsite is south-east.

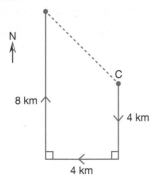

34 Both MOO and ZOO have two Os. You need to find a square number that is a factor of both 20 and 28. This is 4 and so O = 2. As MOO = 20, then M = 5. Also, as ZOO = 12, then Z = 3. This means ZOOM = 3 × 2 × 2 × 5 = 60.

35 There are two numbers less than 3 but three numbers greater than 3. It is less likely the number is less than 3. Statement 1 is correct. There is one 3 and one 6. Statement 2 is correct. There are three factors of 4 (1, 2 and 4) and only two factors of 5 (1 and 5). It is more likely the number is a factor of 4. Statement 3 is correct. So statements 1, 2 and 3 are correct.

SAMPLE Test 7   Page 35

1 C	**2** C	**3** E	**4** C	**5** C	**6** C	**7** E	**8** D	**9** B
10 B	**11** E	**12** D	**13** B	**14** D	**15** D	**16** E		
17 E	**18** C	**19** C	**20** B	**21** E	**22** E	**23** B		
24 D	**25** D	**26** D	**27** A	**28** C	**29** B	**30** C		
31 D	**32** D	**33** E	**34** E	**35** D				

1 As 39 – 4 = 35, Bonnie's favourite number is a factor of 35. From the list, her number is 5.

2 Every two rectangles make a quarter of the shape. This means one-quarter is shaded. Three-quarters of the shape is shaded when six rectangles are shaded. As 6 – 2 = 4, another four rectangles need to be shaded.

3 The boys' ages add to 20 and have a difference of 6. Halving the difference gives 3. Adding and subtracting 3 from half of the sum will give their ages now. Their ages now are 7 and 13. As Joseph is 7 years old now, in 2 years he will be 9 years old.

4 As 26 – 12 = 14, the temperature rose 14 degrees.

5 6 + 4 = 10 and $10^2 = 10 \times 10 = 100$

6 Look at the last three digits. 342 rounds down to 300. The number is 349 300.

7 As 13 + 12 = 25, Y = 25. As 12 + 14 = 26, Z = 26. As Y + Z = X and 25 + 26 = 51, the value of X is 51. Here is the solved puzzle:

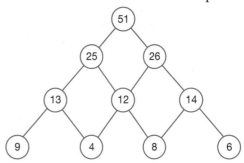

8 Three weeks is 21 days. First, subtract the two days in September. As 21 – 2 = 19, Charlie's birthday is 19 days from the end of August. There are 31 days in August. As 31 – 19 = 12, Charlie's birthday is on 12 August.

9 As 4 × 2 = 8 and 20 – 8 = 12, Owen paid $12 for his carrots. As 12 ÷ 6 = 2, the price of the carrots is $2 per kg. As 2 × 2 = 4, Oliver paid $4.

10 84 ÷ 8 = 10, remainder 4. This means 8 is not a factor of 84.

11 Originally there were 5 × 4 = 20 squares in the grid. There are 5 shaded squares. This means 5 out of 20 are shaded, and $\frac{5}{20}$ is the same as $\frac{1}{4}$.

12 Place 6 in the left corner because the numbers 1 and 3 are small. As 6 + 3 = 9 and 6 + 1 = 7, the top number will be 2 less than the right corner number. Here is the solved puzzle. The total will be 11.

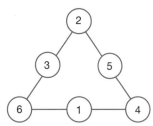

13 Each number has 4 digits. The first digit is increasing by 1, the second increasing by 1, the third decreasing by 1 and the fourth increasing by 2. The next number will be 6549.

14 The sequence is 12, 14, 16, 18, 20, 22, 24 ... Today Greg plans to complete 14 push-ups. He plans to complete 24 push-ups in 5 days from now.

15 26 students read one book and 12 students read three books. As 26 – 12 = 14, the difference was 14. Claim 1 is not correct. 22 students read two books, 12 students read three books and six students read four books. As 22 + 12 + 6 = 40, 40 students read at least two books. Claim 2 is correct. As 12 is twice 6, then twice as many students read three books as the number who read four books. Claim 3 is correct. This means claims 2 and 3 are correct.

16   3 5 9
     – 1▲6
      1 8 3

As 15 – 7 = 8, the missing digit is 7.

17 The rectangle covers eight small grid squares. As 16 ÷ 8 = 2, each square on the grid is 2 cm². By counting, the shaded area covers 28 squares. As 28 × 2 = 56, the shaded area is 56 cm².

18 This spinner has three out of four even numbers.

19 Start with Hermann's result and use opposite operations. 21 × 2 is 42. Adding 6 gives 48. Dividing by 4 is 12. Finally, subtracting 8 gives 4. Hermann's original number was 4.

20 As 120 ÷ 2 = 60 and 165 + 60 = 225, Imogen now has 225 mL in container B. As 500 – 225 = 275, she needs another 275 mL to fill container B.

21 By counting, the perimeter of the rectangle is 10 square sides. As 30 ÷ 10 = 3, each square side has a length of 3 cm. As 3 × 3 = 9, each square has an area of 9 cm².

22 As 24 ÷ 2 = 12, one-third of the mass is 12 kg. As 12 × 3 = 36, the mass of the object is 36 kg.

23 The clock loses 2 minutes every hour, which is 1 minute every 30 minutes. From 9:00 pm to 6:30 am is 9 hours 30 minutes. As 9 × 2 + 1 = 19, the clock is showing 19 minutes before 6:30 am. This is a time of 6:11.

24 The ellipse has two, equilateral triangle three, circle infinite, rectangle two, parallelogram none, isosceles triangle one, pentagon five and octagon eight. This means six shapes have at least two lines of symmetry.

25 As 24 ÷ 4 = 6 and 24 – 6 = 18, Adam had 18 chocolates remaining after Saturday. As 18 ÷ 3 = 6 and 18 – 6 = 12, Adam had 12 chocolates after Sunday. This means 12 chocolates were in the box.

26 There are four squares and each square has four right angles. As 4 × 4 = 16, there are 16 right angles.

27 In the first fold, M is behind the P. After the second fold, A and D are also behind the P.

28 From 10:45 pm to 11 pm is 15 minutes. It takes 1 hour to get to midnight, then another 7 hours to 7:00 am. 10 minutes later is 7:10 am. As 1 + 7 = 8 and 15 + 10 = 25, the time is 8 hours 25 minutes.

29 As 76 – 19 is 76 – 20 + 1 = 57, Rocky walks 57 m.

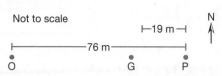

30 The total length is four times the sum of 5, 4 and 3. As 5 + 4 + 3 = 12 and 12 × 4 = 48, the total length is 48 cm.

Not to scale

3 cm

4 cm

5 cm

31 This shape cannot be formed.

32 As 15 + 15 + 10 + 10 = 50, the perimeter of the original photo is 50 cm. As 100 ÷ 50 = 2, the dimensions have been doubled. The enlargement has dimensions 30 cm by 20 cm. As $30 \times 20 = 600$, the new area is 600 cm².

33 From the map below, Elsie is 3 units, or 30 m, from her starting position.

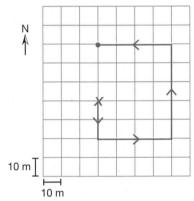

10 m

10 m

34 As $6 \times 5 = 30$, there is a total of 30 faces of small squares on the shape. Four faces can be seen from the front and another four faces from the back. Four faces can be seen from the top and another four from the bottom. Three faces can be seen from the side and another three from the opposite side. As 4 + 4 + 4 + 4 + 3 + 3 = 22, and 30 − 22 = 8, there are eight faces that cannot be seen.

35 Aria received 12 votes and Isla 8 so Aria did not receive three times as many votes. Statement 1 is not correct. As 6 + 10 = 16, Levi received 16 votes. Statement 2 is correct. The number of votes were: Aria (12 + 6 = 18), Levi (6 + 10 = 16), Jack (4 + 10 = 14) and Isla (8 + 4 = 12). Aria received the most votes. Statements 2 and 3 are correct.

SAMPLE Test 8

Page 41

1 A	**2** D	**3** E	**4** A	**5** C	**6** C	**7** E	**8** C	**9** C
10 E	**11** E	**12** E	**13** A	**14** C	**15** E	**16** B		
17 D	**18** E	**19** A	**20** D	**21** C	**22** A	**23** A		
24 A	**25** E	**26** E	**27** E	**28** C	**29** D	**30** E		
31 C	**32** D	**33** C	**34** C	**35** C				

1 $5.00
       $5.00
       $5.00
       $4.80
     $5.20
     $25.00

The total cost was $25.

2 Figure 4 has a perimeter of 8 units. The smallest perimeter is 8 units.

3 There must be 4 tables with 8 chairs and 2 tables with 4 chairs. As $4 \times 8 + 2 \times 4 = 32 + 8 = 40$, there are 40 chairs. Each chair has four legs. As $40 \times 4 = 160$, there is a total of 160 chair legs. Each of the six tables has four legs so $6 \times 4 = 24$. So the six tables and 40 chairs have 160 + 24 = 184 legs.

4 As 11 − 7 = 4, count 4 more days on from Thursday. This means the next appointment is on a Monday. As there are 31 days in July and 11 − 3 = 8, the appointment is on Monday 8 August.

5 The shape has two lines of symmetry.

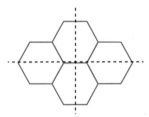

6 As 14 ÷ 4 is 3 with a remainder of 2, she will be given three free bread rolls. As 14 + 3 = 17, Simone will receive 17 bread rolls.

7 $4 \times 6 \times 2 \times 1 = 48$. Two of the numbers are 4 and 6.

8 If James takes one day to paint a third of a fence, he takes a total of three days to paint each fence. As $3 \times 2 - 1$ is $6 - 1 = 5$, James will take five more days.

9   Find the numbers by trial and error. As $1 + 2 + 3 = 6$ and $1 \times 2 \times 3 = 6$, the numbers are 1, 2 and 3. As $2 + 4 + 6 = 12$, the new sum is 12.

10   As $24 - 9 = 15$, the two numbers must have a difference of 15. The two numbers are 50 and 65.

11   Robbie must have been given twice as much as he spent. This is shown as $30 \times 2 + 60 \times 2$.

12   There are 11 numbers in Henry's list: 20, 22, 24, ... , 40. The numbers 22, 26, 30, 34 and 38 are not circled. There are five numbers not circled.

13   As $10 - 2 = 8$, Matthew shaded three-quarters of eight squares. A quarter of 8 is 2, and three-quarters is 6. After Matthew shades six squares there are two squares unshaded.

14   26 students had 2 services and 6 had 3 services. As $26 + 6 = 32$, which is more than 30, claim 1 is correct. 26 students had 2 services and 6 people had 3 services. As $26 - 6 = 20$, then claim 2 is correct. As $12 + 20 + 26 + 6 = 64$, then 64 people were surveyed. Claim 3 is not correct. Claims 1 and 2 are correct.

15   A hexagonal prism has eight faces and a square pyramid has five faces. As $8 + 5 = 13$ and $17 - 13 = 4$, the solid has four faces. This means it is a triangular pyramid.

16   As $16 - 3 = 13$, a total of 13 students went to the beach or the movies or both. As $10 + 8 - 13 = 5$, there were five students who went to both.

17   As adding 8 and X is 13, then $X = 5$. As $5 + 3 = 8$, then $Y = 8$. As $5 \times 8 = 40$, the value of $X \times Y$ is 40. Here is the solved puzzle:

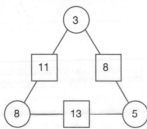

18   The areas are 2, 5, 9, 14. This means 2 add 3 is 5. Then 5 add 4 is 9. Then 9 add 5 is 14. The differences are going up by 1. As figure 5 is

14, adding 6 gives 20. Then 20 add 7 gives 27. The area of figure 6 is 27 square units.

19   $25 + 25 = 50$. The number sentence is $148 - \boxed{} = 50$. Now, if you try 100 as the missing number, you would have $148 - 100 = 48$. This means you subtracted 2 more than needed. As $100 - 2 = 98$, the missing number is 98.

20   As $13 + 8 + 12 + 1 = 34$, the sum of each row, column and diagonal is 34. Here is the completed square. The missing number is 3.

16	2	3	13
5	11	10	8
9	7	6	12
4	14	15	1

21   106, 86, 66, 46 ... is subtracting by 20. The next numbers are 26 and 6. This means 16 is not in the sequence.

22   As $6 + 6 = 12$ and $12 - 10 = 2$, the width of the shaded overlap is 2 cm. As $6 \times 2 = 12$, the area is 12 cm².

23   The scale shows the amount of juice in container Y is halfway between 600 and 900. This means 750 mL is in container Y. Half of 300 is $300 \div 2 = 150$. As $750 + 150 = 900$, the container has 900 mL.

24   500 g is half a kilogram. As $36 \div 2 = 18$ and $36 + 18 = 54$, Alma will pay \$54.

25   $2022 - 57 = 2022 - 22 - 35 = 2000 - 35 = 1965$. Margot was born in 1965.

26   There are 60 minutes in an hour. As $60 - 26$ is 34 and $34 + 12 = 46$, the electrician was in the apartment for 46 minutes.

27   As $6 \times 4 = 24$, the perimeter of the original square was 24 cm. Removing the four corners does not change the perimeter.

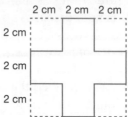

28 This shape could not be formed.

29 A rectangular prism has 12 edges. A triangular prism has nine edges. As $12 + 9 = 21$, the total is 21.

30 The three squares are B4, F5, G1. Here is Amelia's final grid.

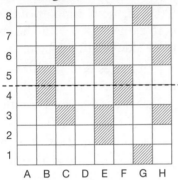

31 There are four small squares inside the large square. In each of these squares there are four acute angles. As $4 \times 4 = 16$, there are 16 acute angles.

32 $13 \times 7 = 91$. There are 91 plus an even number of cars in the collection. As $91 + 6 = 97$, Adam has 97 cars.

33 Both BEE and FEE have two Es. You need to find a square number that is a factor of both 45 and 36. This is 9 and so E = 3. As BEE = 45, then B = 5. Also, as FEE = 36, then F = 4. This means BEEF = $5 \times 3 \times 3 \times 4 = 20 \times 9 = 180$.

34 From the map below, Luke is 2 units, or 20 m, from his starting position.

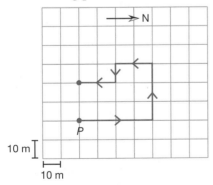

35 As $7 + 5 + 5 + 7 + 9 = 33$, Gianna worked 33 hours in week 1. As $4 + 6 + 8 + 5 = 23$, Gianna has worked 23 hours in the first four days of

week 2. As $33 – 23 = 10$, Gianna worked 10 hours on Friday in week 2.

SAMPLE Test 9

Page 47

1 E	**2** D	**3** D	**4** E	**5** D	**6** B	**7** B	**8** C	**9** B
10 B	**11** E	**12** A	**13** B	**14** D	**15** B	**16** D		
17 A	**18** D	**19** E	**20** B	**21** E	**22** E	**23** C		
24 D	**25** B	**26** C	**27** E	**28** E	**29** D	**30** D		
31 B	**32** E	**33** B	**34** B	**35** D				

1 The number halfway is the middle, or average, of the two numbers. As $84 + 14 = 98$ and $98 ÷ 2 = 49$, the number is 49.

2 Start with Max's answer and use the opposite operations. Add 4 to 12 to get 16. Halving 16 gives 8. Now subtract 5 to get 3. Max's original number was 3.

3
$$\begin{array}{r} 240 \\ 53 \\ +\quad 2 \\ \hline 295 \end{array}$$
The total is 295.

4 As $100 – 27$ is $100 – 20 – 7 = 73$, Emma pays $73. As $73 + 12 = 85$, Zoe pays $85 for her soccer boots.

5 A triangular prism has two triangular faces; a square prism, a hexagonal prism and a cone have no triangular face; and a square pyramid has four triangular faces.

6 As $60 \times 2 + 14$ is 134, the download will take 134 seconds. $134 – 75 = 134 – 34 – 41$. This is $100 – 41 = 59$. There are 59 seconds remaining.

7 Design 1 has one line of symmetry, Design 3 has none, Design 4 has one and Design 5 has one. Design 2 has two lines of symmetry.

8 As $30 ÷ 4$ is 7 remainder 2, there are 7 multiples. As $30 – 7 = 23$, there are 23 cards that are not multiples of 7.

9 The votes were Olivia (40), Noah (30), Liam (20), Elijah (60) and Amelia (less than 20). As $40 + 30 + 20 + 60 = 150$, the total is between 150 and 170. From the options, the total is 160.

10 From the map below, B is 3 units, or 15 m, south of A.

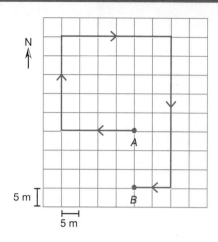

11 As 64 ÷ 8 = 8, it will take eight small cubes to fill the large cube or four small cubes to half fill the large cube. As 4 − 1 = 3, she needs another three small cubes of water.

12 As one-fifth is 20 ÷ 5 = 4, then three-fifths is 4 × 3 = 12. There are 12 spaces being used, which means there are eight vacant spaces.

13 As 12 − 3 − 2 is 7, the middle number on the left is 7. As 12 − 1 − 7 = 4, the middle number is 4. As 12 − 3 − 4 is 5, X is replaced with 5. Here is the solved puzzle:

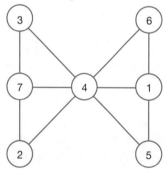

14 As 48 + 12 = 60, then 6 × ☐ = 60. This means the missing number is 10.

15 Seven-tenths of the cards is 21. As 21 ÷ 7 = 3, a tenth of the cards is 3. As 3 × 10 = 30, there are 30 cards in the set.

16 As 46 − 7 = 39 and 46 + 5 = 51, the masses are 46, 39 and 51.

```
    46
    39
+   51
   136
```

The total mass is 136 kg.

17 As 38 − 12 = 26, Sebastian's father was 26 when his son was born. As 21 − 15 = 6, Sebastian

was born in 2006. As 2006 − 26 = 1980, Sebastian's father was born in 1980.

18 Look at the top row and bottom row. The rule is the bottom number is 3 × top number − 5. As 3 × 9 − 5 = 22, the missing number is 22.

19 As 3600 ÷ 3 = 1200, Stella travels 1200 m in 1 minute. There are 60 seconds in a minute. As 60 ÷ 3 = 20, and 1200 ÷ 3 = 400, Stella will travel 400 m.

20 As 36 − 20 = 16, the perimeter of the smaller square is 16 cm. As 4 × 4 = 16, the smaller square has a side length of 4 cm.

21 6:15 plus 15 minutes is 6:30. Mitchell finishes his swimming at 6:50 and the gym at 7:15. As 40 − 15 = 25, Mitchell takes 25 minutes to ride home.

22 There are 20 squares and six of them are already shaded. As 20 ÷ 4 = 5, a quarter of the squares is 5. This means three-quarters of the squares is 5 × 3 = 15. As 15 − 6 = 9, another nine squares need to be shaded.

23 7, 12, 17, 22 ... As 100 ÷ 5 = 20, but 7 is more than 5, there will be 19 students chosen.

24 The number of cans are 1, 3, 6 ... These are triangular numbers. Adding 4 will give the next number of 10, adding 5 will give the next number of 15, and so on. The sequence is 1, 3, 6, 10, 15, 21, 28, 36, 45, 55, 66, 78 ... This means figure 12 will be made using 78 cans.

25 As 12 times R is 72, then R = 6. As 2 times Q is 6, then Q = 3. As 1 times P is 3, then P is 3. This means P + R = 3 + 6 = 9. Here is the solved puzzle:

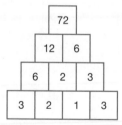

26 W increases the original perimeter by 4 units. X increases the perimeter by 6 units, Y increases it by 2 units and Z increases it by 6 units. Myles should place the paper rectangle in either the X or Z positions.

27 1 has no right angles, 3 has 4 right angles, 5 has 4 right angles, 7 has 1 right angle and 9

has 6 right angles. As $0 + 4 + 4 + 1 + 6 = 15$, there is a total of 15 right angles.

28 Andrew needs to shade P4, P6, Q8, R2, T8, V6 and W2. This means Andrew should shade seven more squares.

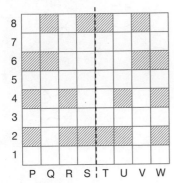

29 $16 \times 45 = 2 \times 8 \times 9 \times 5$.
This means ▲ $= 8 \times 9 = 72$.

30 There are 3 thirds in a whole, and 2 halves in a whole. As $8 - 3 = 5$ and $5 \times 3 = 15$, Agnes makes 15 jumps. As $15 - 7 = 8$ and $8 \times 2 = 16$, Pablo makes 16 jumps. This means Pablo makes 1 more jump than Agnes.

31 Brodie has two even numbers and three odd numbers. He has a lower chance of selecting an even number than an odd number. Statement 1 is not correct. Brodie has a 1 in 5 chance (which is 2 in 10), while Shane has a 3 in 10 chance, of selecting a number between 4 and 8. Shane has a greater chance than Brodie of selecting a number between 4 and 8. Statement 2 is correct. Brodie has one multiple of 5 so has a 1 chance in 5 of selecting a multiple of 5. Shane has two multiples of 5, so has 2 chances in 10, which is the same as 1 chance in 5. Both boys have an equal chance of selecting a multiple of 5. Statement 3 is not correct. Only statement 2 is correct.

32 Adding 3 and 5 means 8 students were aged 12 or 13. Claim 1 is correct. As $5 + 3$ is larger than $3 + 2$, there were more students aged 13 and 14 than 16 and 17. Claim 2 is correct. As $3 + 5 + 3 + 4 + 3 + 2 = 20$, 20 students represented the school. Claim 3 is correct. Claims 1, 2 and 3 are correct.

33 As 6 and 4 are numbers on opposites faces, and $6 \times 4 = 24$, pairs of numbers multiply to give 24. As * and 3 are on opposite faces, and $24 \div 3 = 8$, the value of * is 8.

34 Think about the lines of symmetry. A square has four lines of symmetry. When cut it is possible to form two triangles or two rectangles. It is impossible to form two squares. Statements 1 and 2 are the only possible true statements.

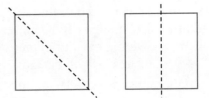

35 The number of laps in the first four days were: Sunday (3), Monday (4), Tuesday (0) and Wednesday (5). As $3 + 4 + 0 + 5 = 12$, Joe completed 12 laps. Claim 1 is correct. On only four days—Sunday, Monday, Wednesday and Saturday—Joe ran at least two laps. Claim 2 is not correct. As $3 + 4 + 0 + 5 + 0 + 1 + 6 = 19$, Joe completed 19 laps in the week. As each lap is 3 km and $20 \times 3 = 60$, Joe would have to run 20 laps to complete 60 km. Joe has not run 60 km. Claim 3 is not correct. Claim 1 is correct.

SAMPLE Test 10   Page 53

> **1** B **2** A **3** B **4** C **5** C **6** C **7** A **8** C **9** E
> **10** B **11** C **12** A **13** E **14** E **15** E **16** A
> **17** D **18** C **19** E **20** D **21** B **22** E **23** D
> **24** D **25** C **26** B **27** E **28** D **29** E **30** E
> **31** E **32** D **33** E **34** A **35** C

1 $94 - 34 = 60$ and $60 \div 10 = 6$. George has six friends who were given oranges.

2 Each square can be divided into two triangles. This means there are eight triangles inside the shape. Two out of eight triangles are shaded, which is $\frac{1}{4}$ of the shape.

3 As $10 + 14 + 1 = 25$, there are 25 students in line.

$$J \; ... \; L \; ... \; M$$
$$ 10 \quad 14 \quad 1$$

4 Two sides of the rectangle are 4 cm long. As $4 \times 2 = 8$ and $20 - 8 = 12$, the two lengths of the rectangle total 12 cm. As $12 \div 2 = 6$, the length of the rectangle is 6 cm.

5 260 – 140 = 120 and 120 ÷ 4 = 30. This means each unit is 30. As 2260 + 30 + 30 is 2320, the value of *X* is 2320.

6 100 – 56 is 44. Half of 44 is 22. This means the smaller number is 22. (As 22 + 56 = 78, the larger number is 78.)

7 As 48 – 36 = 12, you need to find the cost of the additional 12 mangos. If 36 mangos cost $27 then, by dividing by 3, 12 mangos cost $9. As 27 + 9 = 36, the cost will be $36.

8 The number must be odd. The number is not 23, as 2 + 3 is not 8. The answer is 35.

9 As there are four-quarters in a whole, one-quarter of the pies remains. As a quarter of 12 is 12 ÷ 4 = 3, there are three pies remaining.

10 As 12 × 3 = 36, John's children received $3600. As 36 ÷ 2 = 18, then 3600 ÷ 2 = 1800. As 1800 ÷ 4 is the same as 900 ÷ 2 = 450, Jack's children received $450 each.

11 As the small number 1 is on the bottom row, it is likely that the 6 will be near it. Place 6 in the right corner. As 6 + 4 is large, place 2 in the right circle. This leaves 5 in the left corner. Here is the solved puzzle. As *P* = 6 and *Q* = 2, the quotient is 6 ÷ 2 = 3.

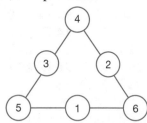

12 Half is the same as two-quarters. If three-quarters is 12, then dividing by 3 gives one-quarter of the number. Now, to find two-quarters, multiply by 2. The number sentence is 12 ÷ 3 × 2.

13 Removing *P* does not change the perimeter. Removing *Q* increases the perimeter by 4 cm. Removing *R* or *S* increases the perimeter by 2 cm. Olivia could remove *R* or *S* only.

14 As 6 + 10 = 16, then *X* = 16. As 11 + 16 = 27, then *Y* = 27. As 27 + 38 = 65, then *Z* = 65. Here is the solved diagram:

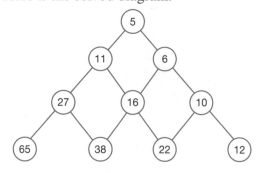

15 24, 20, 18, 17 … The fourth number is 17.

16 As 11 and 4 are numbers on opposites faces, and as 11 – 4 = 7, pairs of numbers have a difference of 7. As * and 3 are on opposite faces, and 3 + 7 = 10, the value of * is 10.

17

```
   6 5 8
+  2▲5
 ───────
   9 0 3
```

As 5 + 8 = 13, and 1 + 5 + 4 = 10, the missing digit is 4.

18 As 21 – 16 = 5, the shrub grows 30 cm every year for 5 years. 60 plus 30 × 5 is 60 + 150 = 210. The height is 210 cm, or 2 m 10 cm.

19 Removing this rectangle increases the perimeter by 4 cm. The new perimeter is 20 cm.

20 250 × 12 is 250 × 4 × 3 = 1000 × 3 = 3000. Rhys makes about 3000 calls each year.

21 If 4 × ● is smaller than 25, the missing number is any whole number less than 7. If ● + ● is bigger than 6, the missing number is any number bigger than 3. This means the correct answer could be 4, 5 or 6. This means there are 3 correct answers.

22 Using the first pan balance, and by deleting a cylinder and sphere from both sides, you can work out the mass of 1 sphere = mass of 3 cubes. Using the second pan balance, mass of 4 spheres = mass of 2 cylinders, which means mass of 2 spheres = mass of 1 cylinder. This means the mass of 1 cylinder = mass of 6 cubes.

23 Tedros needs to shade P4, P5 and U3. Here is Tedros's completed grid:

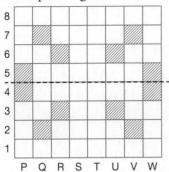

24 There are 1000 g in 1 kg. Two lots of 1.5 kg is 3 kg. Dev should buy two bags of 1.5 kg and two bags of 500 g.
As 2 × 5 plus 2 × 2 = 10 + 4 = 14, the smallest amount is $14.

25 A quarter of an hour is 15 minutes.
As 60 ÷ 5 = 12, a fifth of an hour is 12 minutes.
As 15 − 12 = 3, the difference is 3 minutes.

26 In game A the team scored four goals and in game B one goal. This means the team scored four times as many goals in game A as in game B. Claim 1 is not correct. In games A, B, C and E the team scored fewer than five goals. Claim 2 is correct.
As 4 + 1 + 0 + 8 + 3 = 16, the team scored a total of 16 goals in the five games. Claim 3 is not correct. Claim 2 is the only correct claim.

27 A rectangle has two lines of symmetry. A triangle with only two equal sides has one line of symmetry. As 2 + 1 = 3, there is a total of three lines of symmetry.

28 Three of the angles (*a*, *b* and *e*) are smaller than right angles, which means they measure less than 90°. Angle *c* looks like a right angle (90°) and angle *d* is bigger than a right angle and measures about 120°.

29 It is impossible to make a triangle and a rectangle. Two triangles are possible, as well as two quadrilaterals. Only 2 and 3 are possible.

30 The height of the flagpole is irrelevant. Tessa is 12 m from the flagpole.

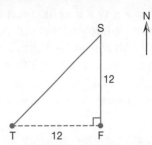

31 Grapefruit is half a symbol. As half of 4 is 2, then two people liked grapefruit. Three-quarters of a symbol is three-quarters of 4 which is 3. This means seven people liked tangelos. As 2 + 7 is 9, a total of nine people liked grapefruit or tangelos. Claim 1 is correct. Mandarin has three symbols, which is twice one-and-a-half symbols for lemon. This means twice as many liked mandarins as the number who liked lemons. Claim 2 is correct. The number surveyed was: orange (9), mandarin (12), lemon (6), grapefruit (2) and tangelo (7). As 9 + 12 + 6 + 2 + 7 = 36, there was a total of 36 people surveyed. Claim 3 is correct. This means claims 1, 2 and 3 are correct.

32 Look at the options: 6 = 3 + 3 or 2 + 4, 9 = 3 + 6, 10 = 4 + 6, 12 = 6 + 6. It is impossible to get a score of 11.

33 A triangular prism has five faces (two triangular and three rectangular) and nine edges.

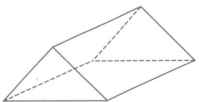

34 The two times are 7:10 and 9:30.

The time difference is 2 hours 20 minutes.

35 As 10 − 4 − 3 = 3, there are three green balls in the bag. This means a green ball is less likely than a red ball to be chosen. Statement 1 is not correct. There are six blue or green balls and four red balls. A blue or green ball is not twice as likely as a red ball to be chosen. Statement 2 is not correct. After a red ball is removed there are three red balls, three blue balls and three green balls. A red, blue or green ball is equally likely to be chosen. So only statement 3 is correct.

SAMPLE Test 11 Page 58

1 A 2 A 3 C 4 A 5 B 6 B 7 B 8 C 9 D
10 D 11 C 12 A 13 D 14 E 15 E 16 B 17 D
18 E 19 D 20 D 21 C 22 E 23 D 24 D 25 B
26 D 27 D 28 E 29 E 30 A 31 B 32 D 33 C
34 E 35 B

1   As 24 – 19 is 5, the value of Q is 5. As 5 + 17 = 22, the value of R is 22. As 19 + 17 is 36, the value of P is 36. As 36 + 5 + 22 is 63, the sum of P, Q and R is 63. Here is the solved puzzle:

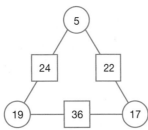

2   As 12 ÷ 3 = 4, the width is 4 cm. The dimensions are 12 cm by 4 cm. As 12 + 12 + 4 + 4 is 32, the perimeter is 32 cm.

3   First, 76 – 48 is 28. On the number line there are seven units from 48 up to 76. As 28 ÷ 7 = 4, each unit represents 4.
As 48 – 4 lots of 4 = 48 – 16 = 32, the missing number is 32.

4   The top row has numbers going up by 2. This means A = 8. The bottom row has numbers going up by 4. This means B = 15. Adding the two numbers, 8 + 15 = 23.

5   As 12 ÷ 3 = 4, there are 4 lots of 3 in 12. Now, as multiplying 4 by 2 gives 8, Olivia uses 8 red beads.

6   As 45 × 2 = 90, the correct answer is 90 more than 717. This answer is 807.

7   There is only one line of symmetry.

8   As 20 – 13 = 7 the cost of one burger is $7. As 13 – 7 = 6 and half of 6 is 3, the cost of a drink is $3. As 3 × 3 = 9, the cost of three bottles of soft drink is $9.

9   As 600 – 6 is 594, the difference is 594.

10   The factors of 49 are 1, 7 and 49. For the other options, 2 is not a square number, 16 has five factors, 36 has nine factors and 64 has seven factors.

11   As Luke has twice as many balls as Jacob then Jacob has one-third of the balls and Luke has the other two-thirds. As 24 ÷ 3 = 8, Jacob has eight balls and Luke has 16 balls. This means Luke has eight more balls than Jacob.

12   120 – 40 is 80 and 80 – 30 = 50. As 50 ÷ 2 = 25, Scott has $25 remaining on the gift card.

13   5 plus P = 8 so P = 3. As 8 + R = 13, then R = 5. As 3 + Q = 5, then Q = 2. Also, S = 2 + 4 so S = 6. As 6 + 5 = Y, then Y = 11. As 13 + 11 = 24, the value of Z is 24. Here is the solved puzzle.

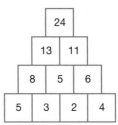

14   The smaller number is $\frac{1}{4}$ of the total and the larger number is $\frac{3}{4}$ of the total. As 48 ÷ 4 = 12, the smaller number is 12 and the larger number is 36. As 36 – 12 = 24, the difference between the two numbers is 24.

15   As 3 × 10 = 30, there were 30 child tickets sold. As 10 + 30 = 40 and 100 – 40 = 60, there were 60 adult tickets sold.

16   The rule for the sequence is multiplying by 3. As 27 × 3 = 81, the fifth term is 81. The second term is 3. As 81 – 3 = 78, the difference is 78.

17   From 20, you need to subtract 5 and then subtract 4 lots of 3.

18 There are 12 rows of 8 students and 7 students in the following row. The total number of students is found by calculating $12 \times 8 + 7$.

19 You need to find three numbers that add to 18, where one of the numbers is 8 and two of the numbers are the same. As $18 - 8$ is 10 and half of 10 is 5, the numbers could be 8, 5 and 5. This means a side could be 5 cm long.

20 As $9 - 8 = 1$, Jack can measure 1 cm. As $5 - 3 = 2$, he can measure 2 cm, as $9 - 5 = 4$, he can measure 4 cm and there is 9 cm already marked on the ruler. Jack cannot measure 7 cm accurately.

21 From 9 am to 6 pm is 9 hours. From 10 am to 2 pm is 4 hours. From 10 am to 1 pm is 3 hours. As $9 \times 5 + 4 + 3$ is $45 + 7 = 52$, the pharmacy is open 52 hours each week.

22 As $5 \times 7 = 35$ and $35 + 7 = 42$, you need to subtract 42 from 68.

$$\begin{array}{r} 68 \\ - 42 \\ \hline 26 \end{array}$$

Lincoln's Border Collie has a mass of 26 kg.

23 10:20 plus 7 minutes is 10:27. As $27 + 29$ is 56, he finished the appointment at 10:56. Adding another 3 minutes is 10:59. (Arriving at the dentist 12 minutes early is irrelevant to the calculation.)

24 From A to B is 5 units, B to C is 4 units, C to D is 3 units, D to E is 2 units and E to F is 2 units. As $5 + 4 + 3 + 2 + 2 = 16$, Mark has walked 16 units. As $16 \times 2 = 32$, then $16 \times 20 = 320$. This means 1 unit $= 20$ m. As A to F is 2 units and $20 \times 2 = 40$, he is 40 m from A.

25 There are three angles. The angles are ticked in the diagram below.

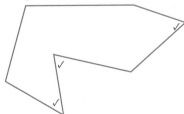

26 Mo needs to shade C2, C4, G7 and H8. He needs to shade four squares. Here is his completed grid:

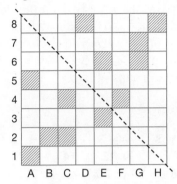

27 As $4 + 1 = 5$, and $60 \div 5 = 12$, the mass of the lighter crate is 12 kg. As $60 - 12 = 48$, the mass of the heavier crate is 48 kg.

28 From 10:30 to 11:00 is 30 minutes. As $68 \times 3 = 204$, then $68 \times 30 = 2040$. This is about 2000.

29 The three angles could be 10°, 20° and 30° which is a total of 60° and so is an acute angle. Statement 1 is correct. The three angles could be 40°, 50° and 60°, which is a total of 150° and so is an obtuse angle. Statement 2 is correct. The three angles could be 60°, 70° and 80°, which is a total of 210° and so is a reflex angle. Statement 3 is correct. This means statements 1, 2 and 3 are all correct.

30 It is possible to make a triangle and a quadrilateral or two quadrilaterals or two pentagons. This means 1, 2, and 3 are possible.

31 A quarter turn to the right is in a clockwise direction. Megan is now facing north.

32 Look at the numbers 40, 36, 32, 28. These are multiples of 4. This means 100 will be in the sequence. Subtracting 4 gives 96.

33 Each of the six faces of a cube is a square. As each square has four right angles and $6 \times 4 = 24$, there is a total of 24 right angles.

34 Six students had two siblings, two students had three siblings and one student had four siblings. As $6 + 2 + 1 = 9$, there were nine students who had at least two siblings.

35 The shapes are pentagon (*P*), arrow (*A*), circle (*C*) and triangle (*T*). The pentagon can pair with three other shapes: *PA*, *PC* and *PT*. The arrow has already been paired with the pentagon and so can pair with two other shapes: *AC* and *AT*. The circle can pair with the triangle: *CT*. As $3 + 2 + 1 = 6$, there are six different groups of two.

SAMPLE Test 12

Page 63

1 D 2 A 3 C 4 C 5 D 6 A 7 E 8 E 9 B
10 B 11 B 12 D 13 D 14 C 15 E 16 B
17 D 18 D 19 E 20 E 21 E 22 D 23 B
24 A 25 B 26 C 27 E 28 B 29 B 30 D
31 D 32 B 33 E 34 D 35 E

1 Square *P* has been split into eight identical triangles. Six out of eight triangles are shaded, which can be written as $\frac{6}{8}$, or $\frac{3}{4}$.

Square *Q* has been split into 12 identical rectangles. Nine out of 12 rectangles are shaded, which can be written as $\frac{9}{12}$, or $\frac{3}{4}$. In square *R*, three-quarters of the circle is shaded but there are also parts of the square that are not in the circle and are not shaded. This means only squares *P* and *Q* have $\frac{3}{4}$ shaded.

2   124
          276
       + 362
       ‾‾‾‾‾‾‾
          76**2**

This means *A* represents 2, *B* represents 6 and *C* represents 1. As $2 \times 6 \times 1$ is 12, the product of *A*, *B* and *C* is 12.

3 The new rectangle is 10 units long and 2 units wide. As $10 + 10 + 2 + 2 = 24$, the perimeter is 24 units.

4 The numbers are in the 40s, 60s and 80s. This means the numbers are 40, 42, 44, 46, 48, 62, 64, and so on. As $5 \times 3 = 15$, there are 15 numbers.

5 It might be helpful to draw a small table to be able to determine the rule used in a pattern of shapes. The rule here is triangles = 2 × squares + 2. So in the shape with eight squares: 2×8 plus 2 is 18. There are 18 triangles.

squares	1	2	3
triangles	4	6	8

6 As $120 - 50 = 70$, there were 70 red or blue marbles. As $50 \div 2 = 25$, there were 25 blue marbles. As $70 - 25 = 45$, there were 45 red marbles. As $50 - 45 = 5$, there were five more green marbles than red marbles in the bag.

7 The numbers could not be 22, 50 and 28. Even though they add to 100, one of the numbers is not half of another.

8 As $50 - 15 = 35$, Thomas bought \$35 worth of pens. As $35 \div 5 = 7$, he bought seven pens.

9 As both days are Sundays, the number of days will be a multiple of 7. One of the options will be a multiple of 7. As $119 \div 7 = 17$ with no remainder, there are 119 days.

10 The squares that need to be shaded are E6, G6, A5 and D1. Here is the completed grid:

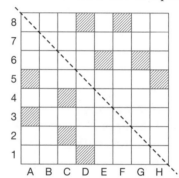

11 Layla: There are 6 columns of 4 squares. Shading $\frac{2}{3}$ or $\frac{4}{6}$ of the grid means shading 4 columns of squares. This means there are 8 squares unshaded. Grace: Shading $\frac{1}{4}$ or $\frac{2}{8}$ of the unshaded squares means shading 2 squares. This means there are 6 squares unshaded. Willow: Shading $\frac{5}{6}$ of the unshaded squares means shading 5 squares. This means there is 1 square unshaded.

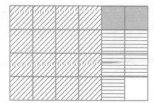

12 As 32 – 15 = 17, the number in the top circle is 17. As 24 – 15 = 9, the number in the right circle is 9. As 17 + 9 = 26, the number in the square is 26. As 17 + 26 + 9 is 52, the total of the three missing numbers is 52. Here is the solved puzzle:

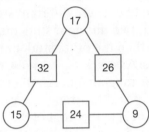

13 As there are 1000 g in 1 kg, there are 1700 g in 1.7 kg. As 400 × 2 = 800, the cans have a total mass of 800 g. As 17 – 8 = 9, then 1700 – 800 = 900. The mass of the cereal is 900 g.

14 As 2 + 7 = 9, the sequence is 9, 16, 23, 30, 37, 44 … There will be six trams.

15 The rule for sequence A is adding 5 and the rule for sequence B is adding 6. The next number in both sequences is 28 but this is not an option. As 5 × 6 = 30, the next common number will be 30 more than 28, which is 58.

16 At 3 am, 9 am, 3 pm and 9 pm the hands form a right angle. This means it occurs 4 times.

17 It is possible to make a triangle and a quadrilateral, or a trapezium and a parallelogram, or a parallelogram and a triangle. This means 1, 2, and 3 are possible.

18 From 0 to 15 there are 5 units. As 15 ÷ 5 = 3, the number line is marked in 3s. This means $A = 9$, $C = 18$ and $B = 24$.
$A + B - C = 9 + 24 - 18$, which is 33 – 18 = 15.

19 As 14 – 4 = 10 and 80 ÷ 10 = 8, the missing number is 8. This means 14 × 8 – 8 × 4 = 80.

20 As 5 – 4 = 1, Emma can measure 1 cm. As 5 – 2 = 3, she can measure 3 cm. As 10 – 4 = 6, she can measure 6 cm and as 10 – 2 = 8, she can measure 8 cm. Emma cannot measure 9 cm accurately.

21 As 5 + 4 + 5 + 4 = 18, the perimeter of the rectangle is 18 units. As 18 × 2 = 36, the scale on the grid is 1 unit = 2 cm. This means the dimensions of the rectangle are 10 cm by 8 cm. As 10 × 8 = 80, the area is 80 cm².

22 First, $\frac{1}{4} = \frac{2}{8}$. As there are $\frac{8}{8}$ in a whole and 8 – 2 – 2 = 4, the other family members ate $\frac{4}{8}$ of the pizza. This means there were four other family members having dinner with Aaron.

23 As 5 + 1 + 9 is 15, each of the lines joining three circles add to 15. As 5 + 3 is 8 and 15 – 8 = 7, the number in the bottom left circle is 7. As 7 + 6 = 13, and 15 – 13 = 2, the number on the bottom right circle is 2. As 9 + 2 = 11 and 15 – 11 = 4, the value of X is 4. Here is the solved puzzle:

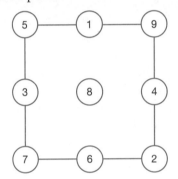

24 The rule for the sequence is adding 5. The numbers are 1 more than the multiples of 5. The sixth term is 6 times 5 plus 1, which is 31. The 10th term is 10 times 5 + 1, which is 51. As 51 – 31 = 20, the difference is 20. You could also use this method: as 10 – 6 is 4 and 4 × 5 is 20, the difference is 20.

25 Look for three numbers that multiply together to give 100 where one number is twice the other. The numbers are 2, 5 and 10. My brother is 2 years old.

26 As 9 ÷ 3 = 3, then 900 ÷ 3 = 300. As 900 – 300 = 600, there is still 600 mL in the jug. As 600 + 200 = 800, there is now 800 mL of water in the jug. As 800 ÷ 4 = 200, there is 200 mL of water remaining.

27 17 = 15 + 2, 28 = 15 + 10 + 3, 22 = 15 + 5 + 2 and 15 + 8 = 23. However, 24 kg cannot be measured using the blocks.

28 This shape cannot be formed.

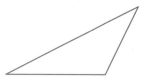

29 Class 4K has four and a quarter symbols. 40×4 is 160 and a quarter of 40 is 10. As $160 + 10 = 170$, Class 4K raised $170. Claim 1 is correct. 5R has half a symbol less than Class 4T. As half of 40 is 20, Class 4T raised $20 more than Class 5R. Claim 2 is not correct. Class 5R has raised $100 and Class 5M have raised $150. As $100 + 150 = 250$, the two classes raised a total of $250. Claim 3 is correct. Claims 1 and 3 are correct.

30 As $8 \times 6 = 48$, there is a total of 48 faces on the small squares. Connie can see 5 faces looking from the front and 5 faces from the back. She can see 5 faces looking from the top and 5 faces from the bottom. Connie can see 4 faces looking from the side and 4 faces from the opposite side. As $5 + 5 + 5 + 5 + 4 + 4 = 28$, Connie can see 28 faces. As $48 - 28 = 20$, Connie cannot see 20 faces.

31 The first time he looked the time was 8:15.

As 90 minutes = 1 hour 30 minutes, the time will be 9:45 when Ross looks again.

32 As $30 \div 3 = 10$, the length of each side is 10 cm. Using the length of the base of the triangle, 5 units represents 10 cm. This means 1 unit represents 2 cm.

33 There are three rectangular faces on the triangular prism. As each rectangle has four right angles, and $4 \times 3 = 12$, there is a total of 12 right angles.

34 Represent each of the students by the letters A, B, C and D. Four different students can be first in the line. Three different students can be second. Two different students can be third and then the other student is at the end of the line. As $4 \times 3 \times 2 \times 1 = 24$, there are 24 different arrangements. Another method is to list all the possible arrangements. Starting with student A at the front of the line—$ABCD$, $ABDC$, $ACBD$, $ACDB$, $ADBC$, $ADCB$—there are six arrangements. As there are four different students who can be at the front and $4 \times 6 = 24$, there are 24 arrangements.

35 Answering three questions incorrectly means answering 17 questions correctly. You need to count the girls and boys who scored at least 17. As $6 + 4 + 9 + 10 + 7 + 8 + 6 + 4 = 54$, there were 54 students who answered at most 3 questions incorrectly.

NOTES

NOTES